DO SOMETHING

Leave Your Mark on the World

DO SOMETHING

Leave Your Mark on the World

Anthony Zolezzi & Kory Swanson

Do Something: Leave Your Mark on the World
Copyright © 2008 by ASM Books
Published byASM Books

Book designed by:
Arbor Books
19 Spear Road, Suite 301
Ramsey, NJ 07446
www.arborbooks.com

Printed in Canada

Do Something: Leave Your Mark on the World
Anthony Zolezzi & Kory Swanson

1. Title 2. Author 3. Self-Improvement

Library of Congress Control Number: 2007942476
ISBN-10: 0-9753157-4-9
ISBN-13: 978-0-9753157-4-3

"Never doubt that a small group of committed individuals can change the world. In fact, it's the only thing that ever has."

— *Margaret Mead*

GO AHEAD.
IGNITE YOUR SPARK...

Pssst...Hey. Hey you. Yeah, you. Let me ask you a question. Do you admire people with a 'cause'? People who seem to have direction in life? Who seem to act with a purpose? Individuals who seem to know where they're going? They're the everyday people walking around with the twinkle in their eyes and that knowing grin on their face. They're the ones who seem to roll with everything, who remain unfazed by roadblocks, who seem to revel in the pool of life. They're the ones who make us ask, "How does he do it all in one day?" "What makes her tick?"

You know the type, don't you? I see you nodding your head. You definitely know someone like that. In fact, I bet you'd like a little bit of what that person's been drinking. Maybe not the whole bottle, but a sip or two. Okay, maybe a cup or two. Okay, the whole bottle if you'd like. Geez. You'd like boundless energy, a twinkle in your eye and a knowing grin on your face. You'd like a little direction and a little taste of empowerment. I know I do. And if you do too, here's what I want you to do. Take the next hour or so. Put everything on hold. Dive into this book. Don't come up for air until you turn the last page. When you come out on the other end you'll be a changed person. The way you look at the world will be altered forever. You'll be able to **DO SOMETHING**. The spark for the twinkle in your eye will be ignited. You'll feel a tug on each side of your mouth gently pulling your lips into a grin. The needle on your internal compass will have stopped spinning so much. You'll see that you, insignificant, helpless, directionless you, can actually be significant, helpful and directed. You'll see that you can actually **DO SOMETHING** and make a difference. *(Shhhh...don't tell anyone, but you'll also start to feel real good!)*

So, go ahead. Keep reading. You'll find **5 Simple Steps** that'll help you unleash some of that potential you've been stepping on for so long. Instead of beating your head against the wall in frustration, losing yourself in distraction after distraction, you'll find yourself actively pursuing something worthwhile. And pretty soon down the road, you'll find yourself encouraging others to **DO SOMETHING** too.

Soooooo, what're you waiting for? I'm serious. The challenge is on. Read this book from cover to cover in one sitting, if you can. *(If you can't, that's okay. We've broken the book up into these neat little things called 'Chapters.' Each one has a focus and a main idea. It makes it easy to take little bites at a time, say, while you're sitting at home doing your daily duty or sitting in class with this book on your lap while you're supposed to be working on a math assignment.)* C'mon now, time's a-wastin.' When you're done, you'll find a page near the end of the book that recaps the steps and helps you remember all the important things you've just learned. *(Yes, it's actually there. You can turn back and find it right now if you must. Would I lie? Look on page 188. Go on. Take a peek. It's there.)* Copy it or tear it out. Tape it to your refrigerator, your bathroom mirror, your windshield. Okay, maybe not your windshield, but in some obvious place where you'll see it each day. Now go on. Turn the page. Ignite your spark. I dare you.

He did WHAT at 6 years old?

WHO: Ryan Hreljac, Founder, Ryan's Well Foundation

WHAT: In 1998 at the age of 6, Ryan Hreljac was upset that children in Africa were becoming sick and sometimes dying because they didn't have access to fresh water. Ryan decided to *'DO SOMETHING'* about it and raised $70 doing extra chores in order to build a well for these children. Others paid attention and began supporting Ryan and his efforts. Since the original $70, Ryan's Well has been established and his organization has raised over $1.5 million and helped build 266 wells. These wells have brought fresh drinking water, to over 400,000 people in 12 countries and helped cause a significant drop in illness. To learn more about Ryan and his cause, visit: **www.ryanswell.ca.**

Table of Contents

WHAT'S ON YOUR LIST?

The people who make a difference are not the ones with the most credentials, but the ones with the concern.

—Max Lucado

By that peculiar look on your face, something tells me that something's bugging you. Yeah, something's definitely bugging you. So what is it? What are you upset about? What angers you? When you're with your friends and family, what do you complain about? What do you want to see changed? I bet you could make a list of things. You know the things I'm talking about. The ones that come up in conversation time and time again. In fact, if you sat down with a pen and paper right now, I bet you could make a list of things in less than five minutes. And I'm not just talking about the little things—like when your big brother won't leave you alone or the co-worker one cubicle over keeps talking too loud. We're talking about big things. Things that have an impact on lots of people. Things, that if changed, could make life in your neighborhood, your city, your state, the country, and/or your world a better place for all.

So what's on your list? Seriously. What's on your list? Take a minute and think about it. *(Stop. Close the book. Stick your finger in the spot where you're at so you don't lose your place. Now, think, for just a minute. What's on your list?)*

And you're back. I bet it wasn't too hard to come up with a list, was it? Good. Now, what's on your best friend's list? I'm sure you've heard a few complaints. And your neighbor's list? And your sister's list? Truth is, everyone has a list because everyone has stuff that bugs them. Yes, everyone. Have you ever met a person who doesn't complain about something? Ummm...no, you haven't. Of course, each person's lists will be a bit different. The complaints will range from small stuff—the constant litter in your neighborhood park—to big things like the rising levels of smog due to the industrialization of our planet. Basically, if you can put a name to it, somebody, somewhere is bugged by it. And most likely, you've heard them complain about it. You've even complained yourself. We all complain. After all, we're human, right. Complaining comes easy. It's natural. Unfortunately, most of the time, complaining's the only thing that ever gets done. A whole bunch of hot carbon dioxide is exhaled, and unless you're a plant in the near vicinity, all that complaining ain't really doing anybody much good.

"But, wait," you say. "I'm tired of complaining. I want to **DO SOMETHING.**" And I say, "WELCOME." You've come to the right place. If you want to **DO SOMETHING,** you can. It's that easy. Your decision to **DO SOMETHING** is all you need to get started. In fact, I'll help you with the rest. Just keep turning the pages and we'll work through it together. When you come out on the other end, you'll be surprised at how easy it was to get started and ultimately, how easy it is to **DO SOMETHING** about the stuff that bugs you. You'll see that you can make a difference. You'll see that it's better to **DO SOMETHING** than complain. You'll feel it in your bones and you'll have a bigger impact on the world than you ever imagined. YES! Little old YOU, the one sitting right there in that chair, holding this little book, can **DO SOMETHING.**

(And the best part of it all? You can be 6 or 106, 9 or 99. It just doesn't matter how old you are. Anyone can make a difference. And, this book is short and easy to read. And, if you follow the steps, it just might make you a better person.)

A SIMPLE PLEA

*(If you've decided, or if you do decide at some point while reading this book, that you'd rather continue being a complainer instead of **DOING SOMETHING**, go right ahead. Complain away. No one will stop you. I won't judge you. No law enforcement agency that I know of will cite you for complaining. But, please, please, please don't leave this book on a shelf or under a bed or in a closet or in the trunk of your car. Instead, give it away. That's right. Give it away. Give it to someone who might like it. Donate it to the local library or a nearby high school or college library. Leave it at a coffee shop with a note on it that says, "Please take" or "I'm free to a good home" or whatever. Just don't abandon it to collect dust somewhere. On that note, if you do continue to read, and you do choose to **DO SOMETHING**, when you're done with this book, please, please, please, don't leave it on a shelf or under a bed or in a closet or in your trunk or buried at the bottom of your backpack with last week's turkey, avocado,*

and cheese sandwich. Instead, give it away. That's right. Give it away. Give it to someone who might like it. Donate it to the local library or nearby high school or college library. Leave it at a coffee shop with a note on it that says, "Please take" or "I'm free to a good home" or whatever. Just don't abandon it to collect dust somewhere. Okay, okay, okay, if you're one of those people who can't part with his/her books, recommend this one to someone, or better yet, buy it for them for their birthday or anniversary or just because it's Monday. You get the point. Spread the word. We can all **DO SOMETHING.** Even if it's something as simple as giving this book away.)

THE WORLD IS A BIG PLACE. THE WORLD IS A SMALL PLACE.

Do your little bit of good where you are; it's those little bits of good put together that overwhelm the world.

—Archbishop Desmond Tutu

Now, before we get too far ahead of ourselves, there's something you've got to understand. The world's a mighty big place. In fact, it's HUGE. For most people, the thought of **DOING SOMETHING** to change the world is almost as scary as facing a two-headed

9

dragon that breathes fire and eats do-gooders for breakfast. It seems out of the question for most of us. Want me to freeze up? Go into the cold sweats? Have my heart stutter? My eyes bug out of my head? Go on then, tell me I have to change the world. Talk about being overwhelmed! That would do it. And for most of us average Johns and Janets, Joeys and Jennys, we don't like to be overwhelmed. We shut down. We avoid whatever uncomfortable thing is causing our discomfort. We ignore it. We put it out of our mind as easily as we forget to take out the garbage on Tuesdays. We take up knitting or finger painting or underwater basket weaving. We crave football season and then basketball season and then baseball season and sometimes even soccer if we're desperate. And in the end, we go back to complaining and nothing gets done. Nothing gets done.

So, if we're actually deciding to **DO SOMETHING** that makes a difference, we're deciding to set aside our finger paints and our remote controls, we're deciding to get out in the world and make a difference, we've got to wrap our heads around ONE small detail. ONE tiny little detail that will make all the difference in the world *(no pun intended)*. We've got to understand that the world's a *small* place.

Huh? What's that? A *small* place?

Yeah, you read that right. The world's a *small* place.

In fact, it's so *small*, it starts inside **YOU**.

I know. I know. I know what you're going to say. You're going to say, in a whiny, overwhelmed voice, *"But the world is a much bigger place. I see it everyday. I read about it everyday. I live in it everyday."* And I'll grudgingly agree that yes, it does *appear* that way, but it's only an *appearance*. It's only what **YOU** perceive.

Now, listen closely. Lean in a little bit so you can hear all of this. I have a little secret for you. What you must truly understand is that without **YOU,**

YOU have no world.

YOU have nothing to perceive.

YOU aren't sitting here reading this book.

YOU aren't seeing things that need to be changed.

YOU aren't able to make a difference.

YOU have no world and therefore,

YOU aren't able to *DO SOMETHING*.

Which is why, my friend, the world starts within you. And it's also why you're making a difference right now. That's right. You <u>are</u> **DOING SOMETHING.** You're reading this book. Just by opening the cover of this book, you've already begun to take action. And this action may seem *small* for the time being, after all, you are only on *page 13*, but you've got to remember, the world is *small*. This world, your *small* world, starts with you, a place where you can **DO SOMETHING** immediately, it's a place where you have complete control and can make long-lasting changes—changes that others will see in you. Your friends, your family, your classmates, your colleagues, even strangers will know something is different about you—something good, something real good. And then, as you change, as you **DO SOMETHING**, the world will become a bigger place and your **small** changes will grow. Guaranteed.

LET'S GET COOKIN'...

Pick up a newspaper, click on your homepage, listen to the radio, turn on the nightly news. The world needs your help. The world needs you to *DO SOMETHING.*

- Tsunamis devastate countries.

- Factory farms abuse hundreds of thousands of animals each day and pollute our lands and waterways.

- Hurricanes fragment communities.

- AIDS continues to spread.

- Pollution—in the air, in the water, on the land —threatens life, kills wildlife.

- War destroys countries.

- Politicians serve themselves.

- Industrialization consumes natural resources at an alarming rate.

- Genocide erases entire communities of people.

- Forests become wastelands, remnants of irresponsible logging.

- Scam artists and pedophiles prowl the internet looking to do harm to others.

- Animals become endangered due to human carelessness and thoughtlessness.

- Childhood obesity threatens the lives of children at the same time that other children starve.

And the list goes on and on and on and on... Bigger issues, smaller issues, you name them, they're out there.

Seriously bugged? Angry? Overwhelmed? Feel helpless? Kinda' makes you want to quit before you even get started, doesn't it? Too bad. You've already started. You've already realized, even though you can't fix <u>all</u> of the problems, you **CAN** make a difference. You can *DO SOMETHING.* No matter what age, no matter where you live, no matter who you are, you can make a difference.

(By the way, have I mentioned there's a hidden bonus to **DOING SOMETHING?** *These issues—the ones that bug the heck out of you, that make your blood boil, that make you so angry you can't see straight—will end up being the same issues that help you become happier and healthier. Yep. That's right. HAPPIER and HEALTHIER.*

"How is an issue like childhood obesity going to make me happier and healthier?" you ask. "What about genocide and war could possibly make me happier and healthier?"

Well, let me tell you. As long as you don't become a gross polluter or start a war or become the next murderous maniacal dictator, the issue, whatever issue you choose, will help define who you are. "Huh?" you ask again. Okay, I'll slow down. Let me see if I can make this a bit more clear. As you work to understand your issue, you'll also, sometimes unknowingly, sometimes subconsciously, work to understand yourself. You see, instead of walking around in a daze avoiding things, you'll be **DOING SOMETHING** *important. Your life,* *maybe for the first time, will have more purpose. And as you work to understand your issue, you'll meet like-minded people who will become your friends, your mentors and your support. Eventually, your chosen issue will show you why you're on this planet. You'll find that the issue, and all the good and the bad that goes along with it, is full of insight. And ultimately it will help give more meaning to your life.)*

Okay, enough about that for now. Does your head hurt yet? Is your jaw sore? I know I've just given you a lot to chew on. Don't worry if you don't understand all of it right now. You will as time passes. I know, I know, you never thought it was possible that **DOING SOMETHING** could actually improve your life. Who would? Who would've thought that the issue(s) that bug the heck out of you, that tick you off, could become a source of happiness and fulfillment? Maybe it's time you find out.

ABOUT THE BOOK

This book has **4 Main Parts.**

<u>**Part One**</u> is designed to be an easy read. It contains **A FEW SIMPLE STEPS—FIVE** to be exact. You'll **CHOOSE** your cause by defining what angers or disgusts you. From there, you'll get yourself **MOVING** with information and outside help. You'll learn to **NETWORK** and begin taking action. You'll **EMBRACE** your cause fully. And finally, you'll be empowered and begin to **UNDERSTAND** how all of this leads towards healing. These steps are the ♥ of the book. If you read nothing else, you'll walk away with the tools to change the world.

<u>**Part Two**</u> is a bonus and can be found in the first addendum. It is a place where you and your cause become intricately linked together in a much

more personal manner. It's a place that focuses more on you and your heatlh and happiness. Here you'll incorporate your cause into a **Personal Mission** statement—a powerful tool previously discussed in *The Detachment Paradox*—and one so valuable that everyone should take the opportunity to create one.

Part Three can be found in BOXES throughout the book. These boxes offer a more personal look at how you'll change the world. These short thoughts are intended for those who are looking for alternative perspectives. Consider them a healthy snack or a delicious dessert. Read them if you desire. Skip them if you'd like. Save them for later if you are so inclined.

Part Four are stories. Stories scattered throughout the book. Stories about people—older people, younger people, somewhere in the middle people, people in school, people at the office, people in your neighborhood—who all share something in common; they all *DO SOMETHING*. These little shorts are examples of how people, in all walks of life, contribute daily. Some started small, real small—without any idea that their willingness to help out might grab the attention of others, while others harnessed the resources of their position to start something big, with the goal of making a huge impact. But all of them, both small and big, are driven by a passion—a passion to make the world a better place. Let's hope they inspire you as much as they have us.

THE 5 STEPS—
A BRIEF OVERVIEW

STEP 1. **CHOOSE.** Choose a cause. You'll ask yourself, "What is happening in the world that bothers me? What issue upsets me to the core?" This 1st Step is where you'll identify and **CHOOSE** a cause. You'll begin to become aware of what's going on around you. You'll pull your head out of the sand. *(After all, you're not* *an ostrich.)* You'll pick a cause. Just one. You'll pick one that speaks to you. You'll take a stand. You'll **CHOOSE.**

STEP 2. MOVE. Get moving with information and reinforcements. Inform yourself. In the 2nd Step you'll discover information that's readily available for you to use. You'll search the internet. Visit the library. You'll ask yourself, "What people or persons identify with this issue? What established groups are already **ON THE MOVE** working on this issue or a similar one?" You'll strengthen yourself and your cause by finding like-minded people and organizations. **MOVE IT! MOVE IT! MOVE IT!**

STEP 3. NETWORK. Participate with your selected group. That's right. In the 3rd Step you'll start meeting people. You'll find ways to

NETWORK even if a local group doesn't exist. Heck, you might even establish one yourself. Or, you might find a similar group in your area and work with them. You'll also discover when events are taking place that you can participate in. You'll put them on your calendar. You'll be involved. You'll **NETWORK.**

STEP 4. **EMBRACE.** Grab your cause firmly and give it a big hug. In the 4th Step you'll ask yourself, "How can I include my cause in my life? You'll learn to personally **EMBRACE** your cause? You'll look for ways to make small changes in your life. And eventually those small changes will lead to bigger ones and your life will be more complete. Mmmm…there's nothing like a warm **EMBRACE.**

STEP 5. **UNDERSTAND**. Internalize the change in your perspective. In the 5th Step you'll

Box #1 The First Box. The box which comes before all others
TATTOOS AND JEANS
(OR THE TIMES, THEY ARE A-CHANGIN')

In our culture, in times past, if you were an activist or someone who didn't conform to the 'norm' you were considered a 'rebel.' If you went so far as to get yourself a tattoo or a piercing, everybody had better watch out. You were walking the razor's edge. Believe it or not, there was even a time, before blue jean Fridays and business casual, that wearing jeans to work was considered a sign of rebellion. Yikes! And throw any of those together as a combination—someone who wore jeans, sported a tattoo, and had a golden hoop sliding out of his nose—and chaos couldn't be far behind. All hell was about to break loose. Can you imagine the nerve of someone like that? The end of the world must certainly be near.

It is quite evident that this is no longer the case. Things have changed. In fact, there appears to be a shift looming on the distant horizon. Shoot, it might already be in motion. The 'norm'—the folks who buy into everything they're 'supposed' to buy into—will be shown to be nothing more than 'sleepwalkers.' Now using the term 'sleepwalkers' may seem a little harsh but imagine for a moment, someone who's asleep and no matter how loud you yell, she won't wake up. Now, take a moment and think about the cause that's bugging you. Why are people ignoring the fact that this is going on? Why isn't it bugging everyone? Well, they're fast asleep, walking in and out of their daily lives without giving much of a thought to anything outside their normal routine, that's why. And even though you yell, you realize that you have to 'shake 'em to wake 'em.' And guess what? You're about to start the shaking as you prepare yourself to DO SOMETHING about what's bugging you. Now, go pierce yourself...or get a tattoo...or don't and just get moving.

begin to **UNDERSTAND** why you see things differently now that you know you are making a difference. You'll ask, "How does my world view compare to what it was before I embraced my cause? You'll begin to **UNDERSTAND** that healing the world *(and yourself)* takes time. You'll learn patience. You'll **UNDERSTAND** that your

---

Box #2 The Second Box. Second to NONE
POWER OF INTENTION

When you make a conscious step, when you put your foot forward because you INTENDED to do so, the energy that develops is powerful. The right person calls. Someone you need to meet shows up just in time. The pieces to the 'puzzle' fall effortlessly into place. This power heats you up, keeps you loose, keeps you moving, and on slower days, it warms you like your favorite blanket. If you choose to wake up and DO SOMETHING,

actions are being felt and that healing will occur. You'll take the time to pause and breathe deeply. You'll **UNDERSTAND**.

if you choose to make a difference, you will discover this POWER OF INTENTION. Not convinced? Test it out. Pay attention to the coincidences that occur, even the seemingly insignificant ones, as you work your way through these 5 Simple Steps. You might notice that everywhere you go and everything you do supports your INTENTION to make an impact. And in the end, you might just change the world and inspire those around you to do the same.

GET READY.

GET SET.

DO SOMETHING.

STEP 1—CHOOSE

to select from a number of possibilities;
pick by preference.

Taking the first step ain't always easy. But look at it
this way. You took the first step just by picking up
this book and reading this far. So, if you think
about it, you've already taken a bunch of steps in
the right direction. So, I guess when you think
about it, **STEP 1** really ain't step one because you've
been stepping this direction for some time. Got it?
Good. Essentially, you've already broken the ice.
You've already begun to **DO SOMETHING**. All you

have to do now is keep putting one foot in front of the other.   .

So, how do you do that? Well, you select a cause. You make a choice. You **CHOOSE**. After all, you've already made it through the preface, the introduction, a side story, a couple of boxes, and the instructions. I'd say you're committed. Not in the put-me-in-a-straightjacket-and-lock-me-in-a-padded-room committed. *(Although you probably feel like that some days. Either that or it seems everyone else needs to be locked up. Don't worry, we all feel that way at times, too.)* Nevertheless, you're committed. You've decided to make a difference, to nurture your inner do-gooder, to rebel, to change the world, to **DO SOMETHING**. In fact, you're changing the world right now through the simple act of reading. You don't believe me? But you are. You're changing your perspective. You're starting to think that maybe what you thought was impossible is actually possible. And in the very near future, you'll help others do the same thing, and they'll move on and do the same thing and pretty soon there'll be this great big snowball effect and...and...You see? I know it's easy to be skeptical. But close the door on your inner skeptic for a moment and consider this. The possibilities are endless! The possibilities for positive change in our world are endless. And you wanna know the best thing? There are others out there who want the same thing or similar things as you. And as you start working on your cause, you'll meet some of these people. Some interesting people who you'll connect with immediately and quite possibly, a few wackos. *(Don't discount the wackos immediately...they may turn out to be a great resource once you get past their...ummm...wackiness)*

Overall, throughout this entire process, you'll have fun. During this whole crazy process, you're going to have a great time. Yes, you're going to enjoy yourself. In fact, it's a requirement. You must have a good time each step of the way. And I know, that stuttering inner whiny voice of yours is interrupting you again saying, "*But, but, but, I'm dealing with a major serious issue here…How can I, how can I, how can I have fun?*"

Well, you just do. I mean, it's true that you're dealing with some serious issues here *but* do you really want to walk around moping about them all day long? Do you want to be miserable? What good's misery going to do you? Huh? Well…? Here's a newsflash. It's going to, well, ummm, it's going to make you **MISERABLE!** C'mon, even if you think we're all headed straight for the sewer you don't have to *act* like the world is falling apart around you. Wouldn't that be counterproductive? Think about it. If someone in your class or your office or your neighborhood starts to complain, others start to complain and the complaining spreads like wildfire and pretty soon it's burning out of control and everyone has forgotten why and where it started in the first place. And, in the end, that's all that ever gets done. A little negativity goes a long way, doesn't it? It's like a virus. You end up with a whole bunch of miserable, whiny, complacent, unfriendly, jerk-o complainers who spread complain-aboutititis to everyone they encounter. And you know what? They all have bad breath. Okay, maybe they don't all have bad breath…but a lot of them do…I've smelled it too often. But seriously though, the worst part, the unfortunate part about all that complaining, is that **NOTHING EVER GETS DONE!**

So, unless you want to walk around acting like someone stole your cute little cuddly puppy, start *DOING SOMETHING*. Seek out people who have something to share. Y'know, the ones who have a spring in their step, a twinkle in their eye, and the 'I'm-up-to-something-grin' plastered across their face. They're a heckuva lot more fun. And after you've spent some time around them you'll begin to realize that the up-to-something-grin is actually action. These people are movin' and groovin', shakin' it, makin' it happen. All day long... each and every day. And their action creates a bunch of infectious, positive energy. In fact, this whole doin-somethin-makin-a-difference-rebellious-change-the-world adventure isn't meant to be negative. No way! It's full of positive energy! You can never really fail when you start to ***DO SOMETHING!*** You can never fail when you work to change the world. The whole process is way too powerful. So much so that once you're involved you'll begin to feel it in your bones because you'll be creating that same transformational energy. And sure, you'll be dealing with uncomfortable issues, serious issues, some I-can't-believe-others-let-this-situation-get-so-out-of-control issues, but you'll stay positive and upbeat about it, even when the going gets a little bumpy. In fact, your energy may dwindle from time to time, but it'll never go away. It's a part of you now. Besides, the way I see it, if you're always walking around holding hands with Mr. Gloom and Mrs. Doom, you'll get nowhere. Nowhere, nowhere, nowhere. And if you've ever visited nowhere, you know it ain't a fun place. It's just kinda drab and grey and foggy. Nobody gets excited about going nowhere…

———————

Who's Greening Up the Ghetto?

WHO: Majora Carter, Founder, Sustainable South Bronx

WHAT: A native of the Bronx in New York City, Majora Carter couldn't figure out why her neighborhood was one of the city's major dumping zones for both garbage and sewage. Almost 1 out of 4 children in her neighborhood had asthma, one of the highest rates anywhere in the country. In 2001, she decided to *'DO SOMETHING'* about the lack of greenspace available in her community and founded, Sustainable South Bronx, an organization devoted to developing an enjoyable, healthy, and livable environment. Sustainable South Bronx has since created the 10-mile South Bronx Greenway, a bicycle and pedestrian path that links eight acres of parkland, initiated an environmental stewardship training program, and developed a business that places gardens on top of roofs in order to reduce cooling costs and conserve water. For more information about Majora and the Sustainable South Bronx, visit: **www.ssbx.org.**

THE BRASS TACKS. THE BARE BONES. THE REAL DEAL. THE CORE.

Okay, it's time. Let's get somewhere. Let's move on down the road now that we've taken a sip from the

FOUNTAIN OF POSITIVE ENERGY**. Time's a-wasting. **STEP 1** needs you and you need **STEP 1**.

By the way, **STEP 1** may just be the easiest of the **5 STEPS**. It can be accomplished simply by asking yourself,

WHAT UPSETS ME?

When it comes to the world and world issues, what really **BURNS** me? Ooouuurrrrggghhh...that burning sensation...

Here are a few fiery issues to get you thinking...

Deforestation, drug abuse, factory farming, war, starvation, HIV, pesticides, genocide, water pollution, animal cruelty, litter, homelessness, child pornography, herbicides, mad cow disease, pedophiles, overmedication of children, cancer, whaling, spousal abuse, air pollution, date

rape, preventable diseases, alcohol abuse, obesity epidemic, avian flu, internet predators…

Whoa…some heavy stuff there…some really heavy stuff. Stuff so heavy that you could take your blanket of apathy, wrap yourself tightly in it and hunker down in front of your favorite reality shows.

Box #3 The Third Box. Box NummerTree
THE FOUNTAIN OF POSITIVE ENERGY

Just by taking action, you'll begin to solidify your place in the movement. You'll begin tapping into a fountain of endless energy—positive energy—that can change the world. You'll feel it. No matter what age you are or stage of life you're in, you'll feel it. This energy just flows. And all you need to do is dip your cup in and take a sip. Once you make a conscious effort to **DO SOMETHING,** to take that first sip, the fountain is there

(Kinda ironic, eh? Avoiding reality by watching "reality"...) Heck, a lot of people wouldn't blame you. But you won't let yourself. You've made it this far. You've got a lot of stuff to do. Of course you won't be able to do all of it at once so you'll have to figure out what's most important. And here's how.

for you and its energy, its positive energy, will keep you focused and moving even on the quiet, tired days. You see, the fountain's energy vibrates at a higher frequency than negative energy and this is why people who have positive energy, people who are **DOING SOMETHING,** are like magnets. They attract people. And the people they attract come from all over, old friends call, people seek them out. They too, want to share in this energy—this life inspiring, totally uplifting positive energy.

First, you'll create your own list of **BURNING ISSUES** and through a simple process of elimination, you'll narrow it down to the one that really screams at you. And it will scream at you, don't worry. But before it can scream, you've got to create the list. In fact, in just over 10 more sentences, you'll find a box with 20 lines. Don't feel obligated to fill in all the blanks. You're not being graded. Don't even feel obligated to fill in any of them if you already know what your issue is. *(In fact, If that's the case, jump past the box and keep on moving.)* If, on the other hand, you're an overachieving-teachers-pet-type and have more than 20 things, write in the margins, write on the back cover, the airplane napkin in front of you, your diary, your algebra textbook, whatever. Anyway, get started now. Oh, and if you feel like you're 'not supposed' to write in a book because someone in your past told you not to write in books, squash that feeling right now. This is your book. Write in it, for heaven's sake. It is filled with paper, after all. It's not a sin. You won't be condemned for it. You might actually be commended for it. So do it. Pen, pencil, blood, lipstick, eye liner...it don't matter. Just write.

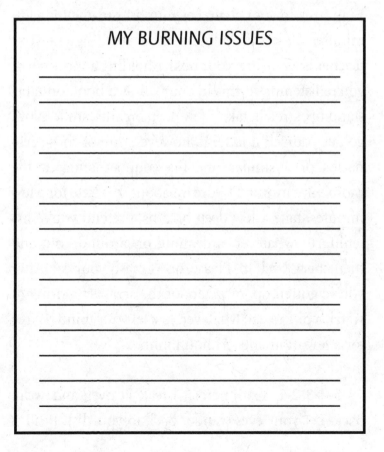

MY BURNING ISSUES

Well look at you go! Nicely done. Looks like a pretty comprehensive list. *(As if I can actually see it.)* Why don't you put the pen or pencil down for a moment. Lean back in your chair. Let your list breathe for a few minutes. Unless the pilot has the seatbelt sign lit, your teacher is lecturing, your boss is holding a meeting, or you're listening to this in your car as a book on tape, stand up, stretch, take a few deep breaths, smile. Now, go get yourself a latte. If, however, one of those scenarios or a similar one fits your situation at the moment, stay put. Daydream about that latte for a few minutes, take a few deep breaths, pretend you're listening to whatever is droning on around you, and then check back in. Please, don't crash your car. After you've gotten up, move about the area, get a drink of water, a bite to eat, whatever. Just let your mind be free for a few moments. Ahhhhhhhhh......

5-4-3-2-1. Commercial break is over and we're back. Let your eyes wander back to your list. Read it slowly. Once you've read it at least once, grab your pen or your pencil, point it at the page and see where it is pulled. And yes, as strange as it may seem, your pencil will be pulled. It'll seem magnetized to a few issues that are consciously or subconsciously important to you. Circle 3 issues—no more, no less. Cross out the rest of them. Yes, cross them out. Just do it. Crossing stuff off a list is fun. It's therapeutic.

Now that you're done scribbling all over the page, write the 3 issues you circled below:

ISSUE 1 _____

ISSUE 2 _____

ISSUE 3 _____

Got your three issues written? Good. Take a couple of deep cleansing breaths and relax. Sip your hot chocolate. Let your shoulders drop. Breathe. *Namaste.'*

Now it's time to pick your cause. Don't worry. It's easy. If you can pick your nose, and you can pick your friends, well…you can pick your cause. Just follow these simple instructions. Hold your pen or your pencil just above your list and relax. Allow your pen or pencil to be drawn to one of these issues. *(No, this isn't witchcraft. Just do it.)* Go on, that's it. Hold your pencil up, read your three issues and allow your hand to move to one of them. It will. Trust me. Now, circle whichever one your hand goes to. *(Pssst…here's the trick behind it. When you allow yourself to relax, you allow your subconscious to take over and it's your subconscious that really knows which one is the best fit for you.)* Now, whichever one you've circled belongs to you. Wahhhh-lahhhh! You've chosen a cause. Cross out the other two. Step 1 is almost complete. All you have to do now is state your cause and what you intend to do.

"Huh? State my cause? What do you mean state my cause? I just identified it and now you want me to state it? But, but, but…" you say. And I say, "Relax. Take another deep breath. Help is just a sentence or two away. I'm not going to leave you stranded. I'm here to help. Ready? Deep breath. Ahhhh…

Now, check out these neat examples.

- I will work to encourage the production and sale of organic foods to the general public.

- I will work to educate people on the dangers of drug use.

- I will work to educate the western world on issues of genocide in Africa.

- I will work to create laws that strengthen the government's ability to prosecute gross polluters.

Now it's your turn:

I will _____

Nice work! **STEP 1** is now officially complete. Go to the mirror. I mean it. Go stare at yourself for a moment. You've changed. Can you see the difference? You've made a decision. You've chosen to help. You've chosen to *DO SOMETHING*. Your momma's gonna be so proud!

Alright, enough admiring yourself. Turn the page.

Get **MOVING.**

STEP 2—MOVE

to take action; proceed

That's right. No stopping. No dilly dallying. No sleeping on the job. You're on a roll now. Keep that change-the-world train moving on down the line. After all, you've just tanked up on some great energy. Can't stop now. You're the 'little-engine-that-could' chugging happily up the hill. Blow your whistle loud! Blow your whistle proud!

So, you're probably wondering what to do next now that you've picked your nose…I mean…your cause. Well, let's see…You can stand around and be angry all day…Ummm, no you can't. That would be a bit too counterproductive. Or, you can harness all that positive energy you've just generated and *DO SOMETHING* with it. Yeah…that's exactly what you must do! You must continue to harness that positive energy. You must continue to act. And that action must include some schooling. That's right. It's time to learn. It's time to learn. It's time to learn. Say it with me now…**IT'S TIME TO LEARN!** So, take a deep breath, sit back and ask yourself,

HOW MUCH DO I REALLY KNOW ABOUT MY CAUSE?

(Okay, here's a cool thing. When you latch on to a cause, you begin to live it. You begin to feel it in your bones, you dream about it, you daydream about it, and you start talking

about it. And you begin to create that same type of energy that I mentioned earlier. You also latch on to one or two big facts that really stoke your fire. These big facts continue to energize you, so much so, that everyone you meet gets told, 'Hey, do you know..." And as you repeat them to others they not only energize you but the people you tell who tell others who tell others who, well, ummm, tell others...)

Here are a few examples of BIG FACTS:

1. Hey, do you know, the average apple has 9 pesticides applied to it.

2. Hey, do you know, a pig on a factory farm never sees the light of day and is unable to turn around.

3. Hey, do you know, at the current rate of consumption, the world will be out of oil in 30 years.

4. Hey, do you know, almost 16,000 children die from hunger-related causes each day?

5. Hey, do you know, Canada clubs to death 300,000 baby seals each year for the fur.

6. Hey, do you know the average local restaurant buys food that travels an average of 1500 miles, instead of buying food locally?

Why all the fact listing, you ask? Well, **STEP 2** is about informing yourself and getting yourself *MOVING* in the right direction. It's time to get educated. It's time to do some research. It's time to collect a few compelling facts that define the passion you hold for your cause. Before you get started, however, realize that you won't be able to stuff every tidbit of info into that tiny little head of yours overnight. The idea is to build a knowledge base beginning with a few core credible facts—maybe one or two or three solid bits of information. Facts that you can use as a foundation that create an impact when you tell them to someone. Facts that you can build an entire database on. You don't need dozens and dozens of facts to get started. In fact, if you fill your head with too many facts you put yourself in danger of losing your focus and drowning in a sea of half-truths and opinions. Don't worry. As time moves on, you'll collect plenty of useful facts. But right now you're just getting started. Keep it simple. One or two or three key facts will do the trick. Now, get on with it. **MOVE.**

"Have you heard the buzz?"

WHO: Howard Schultz, Founder & CEO, Starbucks

WHAT: From community involvement to fair trade practices, Starbucks 'DOES SOMETHING' and continues to strive to make a positive impact in both the local and global community. The Starbucks Foundation works with over 700 youth organizations to improve the lives of young people through literacy. Ethos Water exists to promote access to clean drinking water all over the world. C.A.F.E. Practices (Coffee and Farmer Equity Practices) ensure that coffee suppliers and producers follow guidelines that encourage responsible relationships between farmers and communities along with protecting the environment. To find out more about Starbucks and its involvement in our world, go to: **www.starbucks.com.**

Follow this simple plan:
A. **Find a computer with internet access.** Navigate to your favorite search engine. Do a search using keywords for your cause. Start

compiling information. *(There's a great search engine called 'GoodSearch' that donates money to different charities. You can select the charity you want to support on their homepage.)*

B. Go to the library. Yes, go to the library too. The library has books and journals and magazines and gobs of other resources that your magical high-speed whoopdy-do internet computer can't offer. Ask the librarian for assistance if your library skills are a bit rusty. Start compiling more information.

(Okay, I know this research thing seems like a hassle, but think about how much you'll learn about your cause? You care deeply about it, right? So why wouldn't you want to learn as much about it as you can? Bathe yourself with information. Let the facts wash over you. Once you start to learn, you'll want to learn more. And as you get farther into it you'll see that there will always be more to learn.

Besides, wouldn't you rather be an expert on your cause than an idiot? How awesome will it be when someone asks you a specific question related to your cause and you'll be able to pull it off the top of your head? Much better than that dumb look you'll have on your face when you don't have an answer and begin to mumble and stutter and feel like a big idiot...and, quite honestly, without the research you will be a big idiot. DON'T BE A BIG IDIOT. Too many idiots have already changed the world, and, ummm, it usually hasn't been for the better.)

Questions to ask yourself when compiling research:

How do I know the information I'm finding is credible?

What information really sticks out at me?

Who else is working on this cause?

Are there any high-profile people who sanction my cause? Why do they do it?

How has my understanding of this cause grown?

Do I still feel the same way I did when I started my research? Am I more passionate?

Do I understand other points of view?

Sorry if I'm repeating myself, but understand this: You will be required to wade through a lot of information, research, false leads, etc. *(Remember, ANYONE can post ANYTHING on the internet.)* Be patient. In the long run, all the knowledge that you gain will only benefit you. And as you continue and meet others, you'll discuss your cause at length and continue to gather even more information.

(By the way, be open to views that are different than yours. Opposing views, views that take a different approach, and views you don't fully understand may make you feel uncomfortable or even a little threatened. This is okay. In fact, it's a good thing. These different views will force you to define your own unique approach to working on your cause.)

Speaking of others, as part of your research, you're going to need to track down people and organizations who also work on your cause. So, as you stare at your computer screen compiling information until the wee hours of the morning, ask yourself this also:

WHAT ORGANIZATIONS WORK ON MY CAUSE OR A SIMILAR ONE?

Don't think you're the only one working on your cause. Just about every cause has people devoted to it who have already spent hours and hours compiling information, spreading the word, and beating their head against a wall wondering why everybody just doesn't get it. *(Don't fret if you've searched and searched and can't find someone working on your exact cause. You'll find someone working on one that's quite similar and most likely, these people will be willing to help.)* And the best part about these people? The individuality that they bring to the entire process, of course. Some of them approach their/your cause from the west, some from the east, some from under the sea, and some from a direction only they seem to understand. These people understand the power that an organization of like-minded people can generate and work diligently to bring people together to work on their cause. They understand that there is great strength in numbers. So, as a final part of your research in STEP 2, you're going to begin to strengthen yourself. All you must do is complete the simple activity below. As a result, you'll discover which individuals or organizations are already fast at work on your cause. After that you're free to choose the one (or two) that gives you that warm fuzzy feeling inside, the one that feels good to you, the right one.

A Simple Activity: Read the example first. Follow the instructions after. Now pay attention like the good student you are or I'll have to send you to the principal's office. Here's the example:

Your chosen cause is **ANIMAL RIGHTS.** In your search you have found:

The Humane Society of the United States

World Wildlife Fund

People for the Ethical Treatment of Animals (PETA)

Animal Compassion Foundation

GRACE Factory Farm Project

ETC....

You've spent time on each website, read a bunch of facts and checked out the mission statement for each organization. You know each organization does good work, but which one do you choose?

Isn't this a great problem to have? Isn't it comforting to know that there are other people out there who care about the same things you do? Who have a jump on changing the world? Strength in numbers, strength in numbers! So what do you do? Who do you select to strengthen yourself?

Actually, it's pretty easy. Just like when you selected your cause, you'll be drawn most strongly to one organization. Heck, do the cool pencil trick again if you need to, but my guess is, you won't need to. You'll know. It'll be the one that jumps to the front of your thoughts each time you think about your cause. You'll feel it in your bones. When you think about that group it'll energize you the most because it's the one that's most closely aligned with your belief system. And once again, if you step back, take a deep breath and let little Miss or Mister Subconscious take over, s/he'll point you in the right direction.

Okay, so what are you waiting for? Get going. Get after it. Start working. ***DO SOMETHING***.

The Directions: In no particular order, here are some things to do.

- Learn as much as you can about each organization. Here are some guiding questions:

    a. Why are these people upset?

    b. Why are they standing together?

    c. Why do they do what they do?

- Choose an organization or organizations that approach your cause from your point of view or at least somewhat similar.

- Sign up for free newsletters.

- Subscribe to any journals that the group might publish *(There may be some cost involved but it will be worth it.)*

- Familiarize yourself with the group's entire website—especially their FAQs page.

- Use their 'Links' page to find more research and other organizations who are connected to your cause.

- Stop by chat rooms and/or message boards and ask a lot of questions.

(By the way, you'll find yourself asking question after question at first. It's a necessary part of the process. You'll probably feel naïve, uneducated, and uninformed, because, well, that's what you are. You're a beginner. You're wet behind the ears. A novice. A rookie. You're as green as green can be. But, if you ask a bunch of honest questions your apprentice-like feelings will go away, people will see that you're serious, and you'll gain a deeper understanding of

---

BOX #4. The Fourth Box. Not the North Box. Not the Horth Box.
BE A MENTOR

The most effective way to share your expertise is to mentor someone—a process that will help you as well as another person(s) by reinforcing the skills you've acquired. Beyond that, each day you should act as a cheerleader—someone who constantly strives to reinforce the morale of your colleagues, your friends, your family, your classmates, your causemates. Share your experience, lighten their subconscious loads, help *the cause. In fact, you'll see that people are quite eager to help you out. They'll appreciate your interest and your enthusiasm will give them a nice little shot of energy. And after you work on the cause long enough, other people will come along and ask you questions and you'll be eager to answer them. It will be your turn to play the role of* MENTOR**. *But please, please, I'm begging you, don't turn into one of those obnoxious know-it-all types. You won't be*

release them from the stresses of everyday life and the weight of their cause.

There are few people-related activities, in fact, that are likely to be quite as personally rewarding as providing instruction, insight, and inspiration to a fellow causemate, friend, family member, classmate, or colleague. It is through the act—and art—of mentoring that our connections and interactions with others reach their highest levels.

much fun to be around anymore. People will stop seeking your advice. You'll be all alone. You'll end up living in a cave and well, caves are cold and damp.)

Have I mentioned? One of the best things about strengthening yourself with a specific organization is that you get instant affirmation that the cause you're working on is worthwhile. It also adds more fuel to your fire which creates even more energy for change. The extra energy created will then continue to grow and grow and grow. And not to scare you with all this extra energy floating around, because, well, there's really NOTHING to **FEAR**.** As you work on your cause, you'll actually find that you'll be able to have multiple causes and become a part of multiple organizations. YIKES! Yes, you read that right. At first you'll wonder if you have time for any of this, but soon you'll realize that you're effortlessly a part of your original cause. Working on it will have put you in harmony with yourself and the universe which will allow you to have time to give to other worthy causes. And besides, it's quite likely that these other causes will relate to the one you have devoted yourself to anyway and they will easily flow together.

Alright, that's it. **STEP 2** is done. And it appears that your head looks a bit bigger. You're brain has grown. Seriously. Go look in the mirror. Check out your big brain. And after you're done admiring yourself, let's move on. Let's *DO SOMETHING.*

A LITTLE SECTION REVIEW:

Let's recap:

So far you have: **CHOSEN** a cause. *(and enjoyed the process)*

MOVED yourself into the work of your cause by finding research and organization(s) who actively work on your cause. *(umm, and enjoyed the process)*

Box #5. The Fifth Box. Not a Symphony, although wouldn't that be nice?!

FEAR (The only thing to FEAR is... well, nothing.)

As you begin to DO SOMETHING, don't be surprised to see FEAR rear it's ugly head. Due to the fact that you are heading into unknown territory, FEAR will hop on board for the ride and try to put its arms around you. And as FEAR stands beside you and leers over your shoulder, remember this:

THERE IS **NOTHING** TO FEAR.

In fact, FEAR might say to you, "Hey, if you do this you might alienate some of your friends and acquaintances." It might add, "Hey, you could change yourself, and quite frankly, I like you just the way you are." But you need not listen to FEAR. Fear, after all, is simply

"But wait!" you shout. "I haven't done anything other than read this book so far. That's what you told me to do. I'm sitting in the middle of geometry class ignoring

the negative energy that stops people from fixing problems and growing. It's inevitable, that as you grow as a person you will change and it's inevitable that you will make new friends and lose touch with a few others.

Soooooo...why not embrace a cause, tap into a bunch of positive energy and enjoy the change? You'll become a person who digs a bit deeper into an issue, a person who knows that it's going to take a tremendous amount of energy to effect this change. Remember, all change starts with one person. Don't FEAR. After all, Discovery and Truth are nothing to FEAR. Embrace and enjoy them and watch yourself blossom. You can and will make a major difference in the world. You will DO SOMETHING.

my teacher. I'm on a Greyhound bus to nowhere. I'm in a meeting with my boss. I'm driving for heaven's sake. I'm in church. I haven't done anything yet except read this book. It's all I can do right now!"

And what a good listener you are. Yes, I told you to read the book from cover to cover in one sitting if possible. I see that you can follow instructions. It may not seem like you're doing a whole lot yet, but internally you are. You're digesting ideas, letting things 'sink in', getting the 'big picture.' Besides, by the look on your face, you seem to be enjoying the process. And as long as your boss/teacher/preacher doesn't find out, keep on reading. And don't forget to have fun. Take notes, doodle in the margins. Imagine a world where there was no need for your cause. Remember, fun is a key ingredient. Keep it positive. Keep it positive. Sip from the Fountain of Positive Energy. Ahhhh…Oh, and keep on reading. When you get to the end, it'll really just be the beginning. You see, before every great trip, you always have to make some plans. Consider this the plan making part of your trip. And don't forget, there's a nice little visual reminder at the end of the book for you to create a plan once we're all done. (See page 188.) *(That's not to say you shouldn't come back and re-read any of this book. Do that when you need a refresher, a little 'pick-me-up', or just because you miss me.)* The visual reminder recaps all the important steps and gives you a place to write *YOUR* plan. Tear it out, copy it, make some copies for your friends, I don't care. Most importantly, use it and you'll remember what to do.

STEP 3—NETWORK

to interact with a group(s) of people who have corresponding interests or concerns and remain in contact for mutual assistance and support.

Yes, that's right. We're already at **STEP 3**. And what a beautiful big $\boxed{\textit{SMILE}^{**}}$ you have stretched across your face to go along with your big new brain. The people who you meet when you're walking down the street will dig that beautiful ear-to-ear grin. And you will meet people. In fact, that's pretty much what **STEP 3** is all about. It's sort of a continuation of **STEP 2** which is a continuation of **STEP 1** which is, well, the beginning.

You get the picture. Anyway, **STEP 3** finds you asking yourself,

NOW THAT I KNOW WHAT GROUPS EXIST, HOW DO I PARTICIPATE WITH THE ONE I'VE SELECTED?

Box #6. *The Sixth Box. That's all. Just the Sixth Box.*
SMILE

Smiling allows us to express a wide range of positive emotions. It allows us to show off our positive energy. It is an intuitive behavior. Infants as young as six to eight weeks of age begin to smile easily, even without stimuli. By twelve weeks, babies smile to express joy and in response to others who smile at them. Our ability to express happiness by smiling when we meet others is something we're born with. Smiling and laughing have powerful physical aspects as well. With each smile or chuckle the endorphins that give

---

Time to meet people! Time to make friends! Time to $\boxed{OPEN\ UP^{**}}$ and establish some contacts! Time to learn from others and have others learn from you! **STEP 3** is awesome. It's all about **NETWORKING!** You feed off of other people's energy and they feed off of yours. Everyone benefits. And one of the most

---

us a feeling of pleasure and well-being are produced within the brain.

> "A smile is a powerful weapon; you can
> even break ice with it."
> —Author Unknown

Smiling is a way of communication that all can understand; everyone smiles in the same language. The first thing people read is your face; smiling shows that we haven't arrived with hostility or anger...If you're not using your smile, you're like a man with a million dollars in the bank and no checkbook."
> —Les Giblin

Box #7. The Seventhly Box. The Heaventhly Box.
Do you hear the angels?

Open Up

Let's take a minute to talk about your energy field. Your ener-gy flows at all times. And the great thing? When you're willing to "Open Up" and engage other people on a subject (such as your cause), your smile along with the energy that emanates from you will bring other people to you. They'll come out of the woodwork, crawl out of the cracks, blow in your window one day. You'll be amazed at who shows up. Your energy field, that positive energy that you carry around with you everywhere you go, has incredible power especially when you allow others to share in it. Here's a little exercise to help you tap into your energy.

Try this: Grab a partner*. Both of you put your hands up, palms facing towards each other's palms. Gently move your palms against each other's in a circular motion. Focus on the sensation you feel between your palms. After a moment or so, move your palms a little bit away from each other. Repeat the movement. You should still feel the sensation of energy as it is being passed between your palms.

Pretty cool, huh? It's this sensation that is the energy we all carry with us and spread amongst others throughout our daily lives. It is also why it makes it all that more important to make sure the energy we emanate is positive, especially when we 'Open Up.' One of the best ways to make sure the energy that you send off into the world is positive is by feeling good—feeling good about yourself emotionally, feeling good about the food that you eat, and feeling good about yourself physically by getting plenty of exercise and rest.

*If you've asked everyone around you to rub palms with them and they've given you that look. You know the one. Don't worry. You have two choices. Okay, maybe three, but I'm going to give you two. You can wait until you find a more willing person, or you can go it alone. Just use your own two hands and face the palms towards each other. It still works. It's just not quite as fun. Oh, and if you do choose to go it alone, don't worry that the person next to you is staring and contemplating calling the authorities.

interesting things about meeting all these people is, well, meeting them. No two are alike. Some won't be able to sit still. Some will seem like they're off their rockers. Some will offer points of view that will have you scratching your head. And still others will quietly go about their work giving you the impression that they're doing very little…but…get them talking and watch out. You'll learn all about their passion and much, much, more.

———————

"You can 'Do Something' in just ONE day?"

WHO: Adam Selmon, age 12

WHAT: Adopted from war-torn Liberia, Adam Selmon heard about 'Make A Difference Day' from his mother and decided that he could '**DO SOMETHING.**' He wanted to help orphans who were left behind in Africa, especially the ones he left behind at his old school, the Benjamin Britt Academy. With drum in hand, he headed down to the local park where he sat and played. In three hours he collected $207.00—enough to supply the school with four benches, two desks, and a gallon of glue. To top it off, Adam received a $10,000.00 grant to benefit African orphans from Paul Newman, a long-time supporter of 'Make a Difference Day.' To learn more about how you can 'Do Something' and 'Make a Difference' in just one day, visit: **www.usaweekend.com/diffday/.**

(A quick note for those of you who might place yourself in the 'wallflower' category: So you're a bit shy, or maybe a lot shy. It's okay. Yes, networking for you may be stressful at first. The very thought of having to meet new people may cause you to freeze up. It's alright. Take it slow. Stick a toe in the water at first instead of your whole foot. You don't have to make a big, noisy splash in order to make a difference. You don't have to be that kid in class who's always being asked to keep it down or that gal at work who can't seem to find her way back to her desk because she's always gabbin.' The world needs quiet people. If you look around, you'll find plenty of people quietly going about their days making a difference. You can do that too. And remember, sometimes it's good to get outside of your comfort zone and rub elbows with people you find interesting but may have shied away from in the past. It might not feel real warm and snuggly at first, but the folks you'll be networking with are on your side. They care about your cause too. And you'll see, that as you move quietly about *and begin to network, you and your cause will benefit greatly.)*

Alright, so you're wondering how you actually participate. As with **STEPS 1 & 2**, it's pretty simple. To get started, all you have to do is ask and answer the following questions. Before you know it, you'll be meeting and greeting folks. Ready? Set? *DO SOMETHING.*

1. **Does my organization have a local chapter?**

   If yes, how often do they meet? Where do they meet?

   If no, do I start my own? Or find a similar organization that I can learn from?

2. **Does my organization have an internet chat room and/or message boards where I can interact with other people?**

If yes, dance your fingertips across the keyboard and start interacting. (If not, maybe you can email their webmaster enough and bug them into getting one set up.)

3. Does my organization have an events calendar?

If so, what events are scheduled? What must I do to attend one or all of these events? (An event doesn't always mean something huge. It may mean a lecture at a local university or library or a small rally. Remember, you're starting small and most causes began the very same way—with grassroots organizing. In fact, it may be awhile before your organization can sponsor its own event, however, it's very likely that it will be a part of larger events where it will have a table or a booth or a tent.)

Ladies and gentlemen, boys and girls, if you follow the questions above, you ought to start meeting people soon. But don't start turning pages on me yet, we're not finished. Sure, you might have chatted with someone online and discovered that there is a local chapter nearby, but making yourself aware of all the activities related to your cause should be a hint that you're going to need to **DO SOMETHING** other than just being aware. You've got to include these events in your life. You've got to get them on your schedule. NOW. Your calendar and their calendar are going to become friends. I hope it turns into a beautiful long-lasting relationship. So, what are you waiting for? Grab your calendar. Get this budding relationship off to a good start and ask yourself this doozy of a question:

What events/activities will my organization be taking part in and when are they?

Now, take your pen or your pencil and your calendar and write these events on the calendar. That's it. *(To help you get started, there's another neat little example coming right up.)* I know, I know, you don't have enough time to live your life and participate in all of the activities listed on your group's website. It's okay. No, really, it's okay. Here's the deal. **WRITING STUFF DOWN**** on a calendar forces you to commit to something, even though for now, this commitment may only be a mental commitment. *(There you go committing yourself again.)* It doesn't necessarily mean you'll be able to attend each event. You'll have to figure out which ones are reasonable and affordable for you to attend. So why are you writing these things down, you ask?

Box #8. The Eighth Box. You're behind the 8 ball now.
WRITING STUFF DOWN

You make a powerful commitment when you WRITE SOMETHING DOWN instead of just thinking about it. When you write your goals they become embedded in your psyche and you have a much better chance of accomplishing them. Whether you consciously realize it

Well, having these events written down serves as a constant reminder that there are other folks out there who are committed to your cause. You can't underestimate the impact it will make when you wake up one morning and look at your calendar and see that your group has an event going on. It may be an event in a far away place, but it's an event, nonetheless. And it's an event that's working toward the cause that you have become so intimate with. So smile as you look at your calendar and feed off of the collective energy!

---

or not, once they're written down you start moving towards them—maybe only millimeters at a time, but over time those small movements start to add up.

I have told hundreds of people to write their hopes and wishes on a piece of paper, fold it and keep it with them at all times. I am always overjoyed when I see them and they have accomplished their goal/s.

The Neat Little Example

FARM AID—a group dedicated to helping small family farmers remain viable in an ever increasing industrialized farming environment—holds a huge all-day fundraising concert each year. They've been staging these shows for 20+ years now. Their concerts are held in a different venue in a different city each year. So, the **FIRST** thing you'd want to do is call their office or visit their website and find out the date of the concert *(and any other activities that their organization may be sponsoring, oh, and what cool bands might be playing that day...)* The **SECOND** thing you'd want to do is write the date(s) down on your calendar. And the **THIRD** thing you'd want to do is think about this event realistically. First off, this is a HUGE EVENT, especially if you don't live near the venue. Affording the event tickets, airfare to get there, a hotel, a rental car, and all the other expenses *(umm, like eating...)* involved is a big deal, not to mention, COSTLY!

Many people simply can't afford to fly off some weekend to go see a concert or attend a conference and may feel frustrated that they can't be a part of things. *(Or they may be too young or unable to travel or ... well, any number of reasons really...)* What these people don't understand, and possibly you in this case, is that ***DOING SOMETHING,*** being part of the action, is still possible even without actually attending the event.

Here's how:

1. Follow the action leading up to the event via the organization's website and/or other media.

2. Purchase a t-shirt or make your own and wear it the day of the event. When people ask about the shirt, share your energy, your passion, and your information. *(Remember, you tell two people who tell two more people who tell two more people...)*

3. Listen to a webcast, a simulcast, or a tv broadcasting of the event.

4. Visit the website for updates before, during, and after the day of the event.

5. Hold your own small event (a barbecue, a beach party, etc) and invite others and do your own networking.

6. Do nothing other than look at your calendar and smile knowing that other people are working hard on your cause.

When it comes down to it, whether you're able to attend events or not doesn't really matter. The energy is floating all around you. Tap into it. Walk around all day wrapped in its warmth. And when you are able to attend events, bask in the energy! Drink from the fountain! Quench your thirst! You'll be energized for months on end. And this energy will fuel your efforts to *DO SOMETHING.*

ANOTHER LITTLE SECTION REVIEW:
(Isn't this fun?!!)

Let's recap:

So far you have: **CHOSEN** a cause—something you are passionate about seeing changed. Something that deeply moves you.

MOVED yourself—because this whole process is moving and you are ready to be moved. Ready? Set? DO SOME research. Find some organizations. Prepare yourself to move on.

NETWORKED with others—yep, you're meeting, you're greeting, you're shaking hands, you're working it. Remember how mommy always told you it was fun to play with others? It's fun to work with others also.

And that's about it so far. If you're still reading this book from cover to cover and worried that you're going to miss something when you actually get yourself moving on your cause, remember, the book ain't going anywhere. You can re-read it as many times as you want. It's a 'how-to-book', a reference book. It's meant to be referred back to.

So, leave it somewhere that you can easily retrieve it. Put it on your nightstand, place it under your pillow, set it on top of the magazine pile in the bathroom for those oh, so reflective moments. Better yet, buy several copies and leave one at work/school. One in your car. One in your brief-case/backpack/messenger bag. One in your bedroom. One in your living room. One in your bathroom. One in your...okay, enough already. I'm getting carried away. No need to have more than the one you're holding right now. Just keep it handy. And don't forget to use the worksheet in the back.

STEP 4—EMBRACE

to reach out, pull something close and wrap your arms around it making it a part of you.

Wow, you're at **STEP 4** already. Nicely done. You're moving along. You know, when it comes down to it, there's really nothing better than a good HUG. *(Okay, okay, there's chocolate. And, yes, there's pizza. And ice cream. And avocados. And, and, I'm getting hungry...)* Seriously, food aside, there really isn't anything much better than a warm **EMBRACE.** And you know what? That's where you're at. You've made it to **STEP 4—the Hug Zone.** Reach out, grab that cause of yours and give it one big hug. EMBRACE it and feel its energy. But whatever you do, make sure you don't let it go.

"What do you mean I can't let it go?" you ask. Well, you can't. It's just that simple. To get to this point, you've had to go through several steps.

You've **CHOSEN** a cause.

You've **MOVED** on down the information highway with your cause.

You've **NETWORKED** with others who are dedicated to your cause.

And now it's time to **EMBRACE** it.

Completely. I know, I know. You're going to ask, "How do I embrace it completely? Haven't I already done enough?" No, you haven't done enough and embracing it is simple. You reach out, grab a hold of it and live with it. You take it with you everywhere you go. When you go to bed at night, it brushes its teeth with you. When you wake up in the morning, it gets dressed right alongside you. And when you leave the house, you take it with you. Everywhere. To your workplace. To your school. To your neighborhood. Or your apartment complex. It becomes a part of you. In fact, it already has become a part of you. You've changed. You've changed beautifully. You've developed that I'm-out-to-change-the-world attitude and people can tell. In the way you hold your head up, in the way you walk, in the way you smile, people can tell. You've chosen to take a stand, to do something that helps the world. You've educated yourself. You've met people. And now it's time to take it one step further by making it a part of your everyday life. You must begin living your cause. Grab on tight and give it the biggest, strongest, furriest bear hug you've ever given anything. And enjoy it. Enjoy the warmth, the sense of security, the comfort. Have fun. You are, after all, *DOING SOMETHING*.

And now ask yourself:

HOW CAN I BEGIN TO LIVE MY CAUSE?

Once again, start small. Yes, I know. I've been telling you to take it with you everywhere you go and you do and you will. But, I have to warn you. If you try to do too much all at once you'll become overwhelmed and increase your potential for failure. If you grab this bull by the horns and try to become the rodeo champ without ever having been on a bull before, you just might get thrown off. And we don't want that. We don't want you broken, bloodied and blue. OUCH! So yes, I want you to live your cause and make it a part of your life, just don't go overboard. Don't turn into crazy obsessed uh-oh-here-comes-nutty-Mary-on-her-change-the-world-horse. You've met Mary before, or her counterpart, Marty.

They're the ones people back away from, change direction when they see them coming, make excuses to get away. I don't want you obsessed. You've got to have some balance. You've got to remain objective. Without balance, without objectivity, you will crash and burn. You'll end up on your couch wrapped back up in your blanket of $\boxed{\textbf{\textit{APATHY}}^{**}}$ mindlessly flipping from one show to the next. This whole process is going to take some time. You don't want to scare your friends and family away. And you definitely don't want to scare yourself away.

Alright, now that I've begged you to remain balanced, let's get back to your question:
How can I begin to *live* my cause?

Instead of waxing on poetically about ways you might do this or do that, I'm going to jump in with a more direct approach. Let's pretend your cause is *THE ENVIRONMENT.* And let's start living your cause only at home. *(In order to keep that precious balance I mentioned earlier...of course.)*

You can begin to live your cause in your home by...

1. Making yourself aware of your water usage.

2. Making yourself aware of your gas and electric usage.

Box #9. The Ninth Box. The three times three box.
APATHY BLOWS

Apathy isn't something an I'm-out-to-change-the-world-person ever really embraces. A strong focus on the cause and a positive attitude don't leave much room for apathy. Sure, you'll deal with some setbacks. When you drive down a road full of POTHOLES,** fall flat on your face, slip on a banana peel, take the right

3. Recycling.

4. Reusing.

5. Reducing your waste by using a thermos for coffee, reading your news online, using cloth napkins, washable kitchen towels, etc.

6. Purchasing organic food which promotes sustainable farming.

---

turn instead of the left, get lost in the forest, or land in a spot you didn't want to be in, you'll pick yourself up, dust yourself off, re-orient yourself, re-energize yourself with a renewed focus on your cause and keep on moving. You won't head home to sit on your couch and eat bon-bons. That would be quitting and well, you're obviously not a quitter if you're still reading this book.

7. Bicycling the mile or two to the store instead of driving.

8. Driving a more energy efficient automobile.

I could continue on with this list. I could have you composting all your organic material, planting your own organic garden, capturing rainwater run-off, saving your greywater for future use, brewing up your own bio-diesel in the garage, gardening on your roof, etc, etc, etc. But we'd be going overboard. Not that any of those things are bad things. But they are a bit more advanced. They are things to shoot for down the road once the other things have become such a part of your regular habit that you don't even realize it, but not yet. You can **EMBRACE** things and still have balance.

So, let's start with that first little hug. Let's do a little work. Grab that pen or pencil again. Make a quick list of 5 things you can do at your home that relate to your cause. Don't go overboard. Be creative if you need to be. Depending on your cause, these 5 things might not jump right off the top of your head. Remember, however, that a lot of causes are related so doing something at home that doesn't seem directly related, but is closely related, is okay. It's fine. It's good. In fact, to get started, you may have to do things at home that are a little more

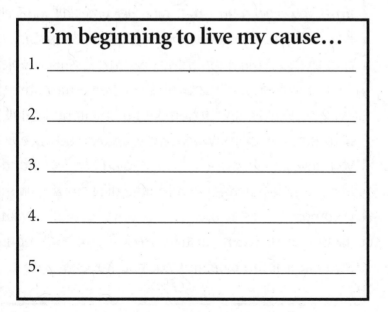

I'm beginning to live my cause...

1. _____

2. _____

3. _____

4. _____

5. _____

Box #10. The Tenth Box. Part of the Top Ten Countdown!

POTHOLES

As you walk, or drive, or ride your bike through life, as you do your best to DO SOMETHING, it is inevitable that at times you'll stumble or fall or run into potholes. Those sometimes small, sometimes crater-sized potholes are a part of life. Sometimes you scrape your knee, sometimes you muddy your clothes, and other times you blow a tire. And still other times all you feel is a little jolt. Try as you might to fill in the potholes and to avoid them off in the distance, it is inevitable that you will stumble through them from time to time. The key to dealing with potholes, both big and small, is to not fear them. Whenever you come across one, you have to ask yourself, "Why should I let fear stand in my way? It's only a pothole, after all. I can deal with a pothole. I can step over it. I can drive around it. I can jump over it. I can fill it in. Heck, I can walk right through it if I'm careful. I will not, however, fear it."

Remind yourself, fear is not you. Fear, often times, is a result of someone else's control dramas that have been beaten into you from a previous generation.

Is all fear bad? Not when we take a look at it from a different perspective. Like, what happens if we keep polluting our planet? In fact, maybe a new 'fear' is what we need. Like we'd better get out of our recliners and DO SOMETHING or we're going to self-destruct. We must understand that journeys are often times long, broken roads, especially those that pose many challenges—the kinds of challenges that tap into our fears and steer us into momentum sapping potholes. But we also must realize that the problems we're trying to fix, although they may pose significant obstacles, are worthy of our time and ultimately fixable. So, get out in the middle of the road, deal with the potholes, do something worthwhile and remember, people who never get onto the road always avoid the potholes.

indirectly related to your cause. You can't, after all, grab a sponge and some dish soap, hop on a plane in the next five minutes and head to the latest oil spill. *(Well, maybe you can, but I can't)* But you can make sure that the used oil in your car gets recycled properly. You may not be able to grab your hoe and lend a hand at the organic farm in Smallsville, Iowa, but you can incorporate more organic foods into your diet. What I'm trying to get at, is that it's okay if it takes a little creativity to feel like you're embracing your cause as long as you make the conscious effort to **DO SOMETHING**.

Hey, not bad. Are you sure you spelled everything correctly up there? Just kidding. I half a hard time spelling somechimes two. Okay, enough with the Spelling Bee. Sorry, I lose focus once in awhile. Back to the list… Once you **EMBRACE** your cause and **TAKE ACTION**** by implementing a few simple things from your list, you'll begin to live your cause.

And as time moves along, you'll start seeing other things that can be done and your list of 5 will naturally, almost effortlessly grow. You remember the advanced list, don't you? And when you talk with your family and friends and they see that you're making changes, they'll make changes too. And their friends and families will make changes too. And pretty soon your small changes, the ones that may seem insignificant—like recycling your used motor oil instead of dumping it down a drain or into the garbage so that it finds its way into the water sytems—are being done by many and the impact on your community and our world, has grown much larger. Pretty cool, huh?! Your big little bear hug has turned into one big group bear hug!

And that's it for **STEP 4**. Enter the **HUG ZONE**. It's pretty simple. Give yourself and the world a bear hug. Put things in motion, make your cause a part of your life. Sooner, rather than later, you'll be making

Box #11. The Eleventh Box. Not the Eleventh Hour.
We're talkin' boxes, not time.

TAKE ACTION

Once you begin to take action, it becomes powerful. Energy starts flowing through you. You feel empowered. Your whole attitude changes because instinctively you've always known you could **DO SOMETHING**. You've always known you could help change the world and now you are. You'll start to realize that you're making a difference— each day, each moment—and it feels good! People don't realize how powerful a few small steps can be. Taking small steps many, many times is all it takes. And no, it's not always rational. Often times—when you think about causes and people making a difference—very few of them knew what or how they were going to go about making a difference. They just started down a path and the path led to people and situations where they could grow and continue to exhibit their passions.

Many people may think you're a bit 'wacked' but by knowing your cause deeply resonates within you, you will remain grounded. And being grounded makes you powerful. You can absorb the big outside shocks and keep moving. Others will see it in you. They'll feel it emanating from you. But most importantly, you will know it. You will be 'powerful' without realizing how powerful.

For Anthony (one of the co-authors of the book you have in your hands), as he continues to get more and more immersed into the organics and sustainable farming movement, more and more people come to support his efforts either by reinforcing what he already knows and making it stronger or just by giving him the moral support to keep going. He keeps tapping into the fountain. Sometimes he even goes skinny-dipping in it!

more and more and more changes and these changes will become infectious! You'll constantly be ***DOING SOMETHING***, sometimes without even knowing it. And it'll be something worthwhile, something that gives back, something that is good for the soul. Enjoy the process. **EMBRACE IT!**

AND YET, ANOTHER LITTLE SECTION REVIEW: *(You can't wait. I know it.)*

Let's recap a third time: *(But who's counting?)*

So far you have: **CHOSEN** a cause—if you could marry your cause, you would. It's been waiting for you it's whole life.

MOVED yourself—not in the box up all your worldly possessions, place them in a truck, and drive down the street. No. More like intellectually and emotionally. You've educated yourself. Gotten yourself ready.

NETWORKED with others—not in the I.T. sense of networking. Nope. You're actually working with others. And you enjoy it. You're inspired by them. You like them. And it's nice. Real nice.

EMBRACED your cause—it has moved in. You have a new room-mate. Get to know him/her/it. He/she/it's going to be around for a long time. Keep it close. Hold it tight. HUG IT, BABY, HUG IT!

I'll stop with all of the hullabaloo about you just sitting there, doing nothing other than read-ing the book, etc. Just keep keeping on. Read.

Internalize the information, understand the steps, and come back to them. Besides, it's healthy practice to do a complete overview of a project before you begin one. Continue overviewing. You are, after all, still ***DOING SOMETHING.***

(Sorry, I can't send you on to the 5th Step just yet. Gotta make something a little more clear. Let's say you're a working parent. You've got two kids at home. You're busy. You can't drop everything and make your cause your life. You can't even come close but you still want to help out. You want to feel like you're contributing. So, you've started doing your 5 little things at home, you're seeing a difference in yourself and your family, but you're still not feeling like you're doing much for the world. You're wondering how your little things are making an impact.

Let's go back to the beginning of the book. Remember when we talked about the world, your world, starting within you? Remember that? And how we should start small? That's what you're doing. The little changes you make change the way you live. And your changes have an impact on others around you—your kids, your spouse, etc. (Who, by the way, talk to their friends and family too.) No, you might not see immediate results, but the person you have over for dinner may go home thinking, 'Hey, I wonder if she's onto something? I wonder if I can do that too?' Remember, change takes time, sometimes a heck of a lot of time. Be patient. What's it going to hurt by making a few changes around the house, anyway? You can be certain, however, that not incorporating things into your life will change nothing. And nothing isn't really what we're shooting for here, is it?)

STEP 5—UNDERSTAND

*to have full knowledge of; to completely grasp
an idea(s) and/or a situation(s)*

Is anybody having any fun yet? I said, "IS ANYBODY HAVING ANY FUN YET?" If not, you should be. Enjoy all of it! Have fun! Let your hair down! Let it all hang out! March to the beat of your own little drum, drum, drum! If you haven't started having fun, do it now or I'll, I'll, I'll...Well, I'm not really sure what I'll do. So just have fun. Keep it positive. Keep it fun. Positive energy infects others with positive energy who infect others who infect others who infect, well, you get the picture. It's a virus we all should catch!

So how's it all going so far? It all makes sense, doesn't it?

You **CHOSE** a cause.

You **MOVED** yourself into your cause with info and contacts.

You **NETWORK** with others.

You **EMBRACE** your cause.

And finally,   You'll **UNDERSTAND** it all.

Bet you didn't think things could be this simple, did you? When it comes down to it, these steps are all about making a conscious decision to stop walking around in your own little the-world-revolves-around-me bubble. These steps force you to become part of your world. *"But I am part of my world and I have been since the day I was born,"* you whine. Well, yes. We're all physically a part of this world *(Well, except for maybe my cousin Bob.)* We all inhabit this space together, but many of us lock ourselves up in our own little spaces and continue to 'live' in our 'own little worlds.' In fact, a recent study* conducted between the University of Arizona and Duke University confirms this. It revealed that friendship in America has significantly dwindled in the past 20 years. In other words, people stick to themselves. *(Hey, maybe Friendship could be your cause. It is important, after all. We all need friends. Someone whose nose we can...ahhh, never mind.)* You know. You've done it. You drive around with blinders on. You go from work or

---

* McPherson, Miller, L. Smith-Lovin, M. Brashears, Social Isolation in America: Changes in Core Discussion Networks over Two Decades, American Sociological Review, 2006, Vol. 71, (June: 353-375)

school to home and back automatically. You yell at the driver in front of you, get impatient in the grocery aisle because the lady in front of you can't find her ATM card, go home, eat the same dinner and watch the same television programs. You have lived in your 'own little world' and so has your neighbor and the folks across town and in the next state over. At some point in time, you've probably even muttered, 'Oh, Suzy/Jim/Theresa/Henry/Beatrice/Martin/Mindy/Gabriel/June/Joey lives in her/his own little world…"

'Living in your own little world happens. Let's not make excuses about it. Let's not judge it. Let's just say, it happens and move on. Oh wait, you've already moved on! You've chosen to take part. You've reached **Step 5**, for heaven's sake. You've chosen to be a part of this world—our world. You've chosen to make changes! Welcome! We've been waiting for you to stick a big needle in your bubble and burst free. And now, NOW it's time to feel the power that those changes have created and will continue to create as time passes.

So here it goes. I'll stop blabbering and get on with it. Step 5 is a bit more in-depth than the other steps. You have three 'Little Things' to do.

These things:

a) give you a quick view of your mental and physical well-being,

b) check the progress you've made, and finally

c) offer you a sense of acceptance.

Ultimately, when it comes down to it, we can bunch all of the Step 5 exercises together and call them UNDERSTANDING.

Little Thing 1: Check your emotions.

The first part of **Step 5** is an emotional check. Don't worry. No need to set up an appointment at the psychologist's. *(Unless of course you want to.)* All you're doing is taking a quick gut check. You see, we all need to stop and reflect, check our feelings, check our heads. So, sit back, take a few deep breaths and check out these questions. They'll help you check the pulse of your cause. By the way, it's okay to take a moment and answer them. However, if you're reading this book in one sitting, dog-ear this page *(Go ahead, bend the little corner over. It's okay. Really.)* and come back to it after you've begun to ***DO SOMETHING*** other than read, change your perspective, get all fired up about a cause, etc. Okay, so here are the questions.

- *How do you feel now that you've started making a difference and begun changing the world?*

- *In terms of your cause and the progress you have made, how's it all going?*

- *How does all of this work make you feel? How do you feel both physically and mentally, in general?*

- *What have you learned so far?*

- *How many people have you told about your cause?*

- *What have you done at home/work/school/etc. to begin living your cause?*

So far, maybe you've done a little, maybe you've done a lot. Maybe you're still sitting in the same place you were sitting when you picked up this book. *(If so, I know you're making plans...)* The fact is, you've moved on and you're approaching THE FINISH LINE. In fact, if you followed instructions, so far all you've really done is read. But is that really all you've done? **STEPS 1-4** have impacted you in one way or another. And if you've gotten to this point, you're definitely moving in the I'm-gonna-change-the-world direction. **STEP 5** will always be here as a gut check whether you're sitting back at the computer doing research in the early steps or after you've gotten yourself really involved. And now that you've got this page dog-eared, it'll be easy to stop and take a break, take a deep breath and look around to see what you've done, to look where you're heading and **REFLECT**** on where you've been.

And let's think about it. Let's say you're working on this cause, you're excited about it, you're moving forward with it, you're talking to people about it. How many **PEOPLE HAVE YOU HAD AN IMPACT ON?**** How many lives have you touched without even knowing it? Many more people than you know because the people you have told have gone off into their worlds and shared your energy. Seriously, when you tell someone about your cause you have initiated change. It's that simple. That's the amazing thing about taking steps to change the world. The universe wants you to succeed so the process of changing the world becomes effortless. By being true to your cause and ultimately your inner self, you create change. When you speak, people believe you. They become inspired by your passion. They become empowered to make a difference also. Heck, if _you_ can change the world, anyone can, right?! And it's never a control issue. It's never a 'You-must-eat-an-all-organic-vegan-diet-and-walk-barefoot-daily-through-the-grass-while-chanting-'I hate all motor vehicles' thing. You concern yourself with yourself and your passion. That's enough. People will be attracted to who you are and what you do. And sure, you might argue passionately about why your cause is necessary, but it's never about control. You're not trying to tell someone they have to do something. That tactic never works.

People like to *REBEL* too much. You see, it's always about the beauty of your cause and this beauty has a tremendous amount of positive energy that will sweep people up and move them along. Overall, it's a wonderful thing.

Little Thing 2: What do you see?

When you look outside of yourself and begin nosing about in the world, what do you see? And, how do you see? Are you too emotionally involved with every-

---

Box #12. *The Twelfth Box. An even dozen.*
REFLECT

Stepping back and taking time to feel who you are and what you stand for and what your beliefs are is extremely important. Doing this often as you move down the path of life is important. Some people refer to it as meditation. Whatever you choose to call it, it's essentially a quiet time of reflection. This can be done

thing that is going on around you or are you able to step back, be objective and remain $\boxed{\textit{DETACHED**}}$? Before you began reading this book, before you selected a cause, did you look at things differently? The next big question with **Step 5** is:

How do you view the world?

Over the past few years a message has gone out. Be yourself. Be all about you. March to the beat of your

---

on a walk, a rest in a chair or lying down on the floor. When you are making changes and stirring things up, reflection or looking at yourself from afar is vital. It not only helps to keep you grounded and uplifted simultaneously, but it empowers you to continue, to push on because fear cannot overcome someone who takes the time to focus on being who they are and not what someone else tells them to be.

own drum. Act differently, etc. etc. etc. The message has been very focused on the individual, which, in one respect is okay. We all need to be ourselves and guide our own ship. We all need to be able to put on our own oxygen masks on before we help someone else. Unfortunately, many people have taken that message as, "I'm the only one who matters. I'm going to go and do what I want to do, when I want

---

Box #13. The Thirteenth Box. The teenager.
YOUR IMPACT ON OTHERS

We talked about positive energy and how it creates more positive energy. We talked about how a smile—the universal language—allows others to know you're up to something good and how it allows you to spread your positive energy around. We cannot stress how important your effect on others is. YOU are a being with a cause and whether or not people actually know you have a cause doesn't necessarily matter. You

to do it, and I don't care about anybody else." *(For more information on this, check out the results of a 20+ year long study on narcissism headed by Professor Jean Twenge of San Diego State University. It's pretty darn interesting.)* We've become very ME focused. We've gone and done what satisfies ME and only ME. It's actually rather sad when you think about it. We've been dependent on each other for survival for centuries *(and we still are)*,

impact others with your positive energy—everyday. From the clerk at your 'Daily Grind' who pours your coffee to the security guard at your office, people are attracted to your positive energy. Your magnetic energy pulls people towards you. You're a positive energy 'pinball' bouncing around and the more you bounce, the more energy you pick up and the more people you impact. Your 'personal effect' grows and grows as you meet more people and more people feel your energy. It happens and it's a beautiful thing to watch.

but cut me off on the freeway and I'll tell you and your mother a thing or two. Spend a little too much time chatting with the clerk at the supermarket and someone might give you an ear full for wasting their precious time. We've become self-absorbed to a fault. We've slashed. We've burned. We've taken without giving much back and it's now time we took responsibility for our actions. It's time to set some things right. So let's get back to the question. At some point in your life, you've probably been rather self-

---

Box #14. The Fourteenth Box. Two Number 7s. Not 007
DETACHMENT

The ability to stand outside of a situation—to DETACH from it emotionally—is both powerful and necessary if you plan on keeping yourself centered as you involve yourself with a cause. It allows you to invest yourself fully into the task at hand without trying to control other people's thoughts or actions. It allows you to

absorbed. Now, however, you're not. How do we know?

You're still here. You haven't closed the book yet and left it at the coffee shop. It's obvious you want to make a difference. $\boxed{YOU^{**}}$ want to feel better about your place in the world. $\boxed{YOU^{**}}$ want to *DO SOME-THING.* $\boxed{YOU^{**}}$ want to change the world. And as cool as it might be to end up on the cover of TIME magazine, you're not doing it for accolades. You're

---

understand that no matter how hard you try to control others and/or the entire situation, you'll simply end up frustrated and angry because it will never happen. You can only control your actions and reactions. Ultimately, being detached allows you to stay focused. It allows you to continue to tap into the positive energy of your cause. It allows you to DO SOMETHING without all the other junk that others might bring to the table.

doing it because it's the right thing to do. And yes, if you look deep enough into what you are doing, you'll find an interesting paradox regarding helping the world and helping yourself and being self-absorbed and unself-absorbed but it's okay. It's okay because ultimately your heart is in the right place and even if you do end up on the cover of a magazine, you'll have gotten there for *DOING SOMETHING* good. For *DOING SOMETHING* that makes our planet a better place for all

---

Box #15. *The Fifteenth Box. Time to get your driver's permit.*
YOU, YOU, YOU

YOU *have a cause which gives you a purpose and a mission*

YOU *feel good about having a cause and what you are doing for the world. This is positive energy.*

YOU *are serving others—each moment, each place you go, and each person you touch.*

mankind. And you won't have had to sell your soul to get there. Pretty cool, huh?

Eco...what?

WHO: Jeffrey R. Immelt, CEO, General Electric

WHAT: In 2005, with CEO, Jeff Immelt leading the way, General Electric, showed the world that it could '*DO SOMETHING*' by launching Ecomagination, an innovative initiative to help green the planet by developing energy efficient and environmentally-friendly products that help companies not only control their energy overhead, but also cut their emissions. At the same time, GE set itself up as an example for other companies by implementing over 500 global energy conservation projects and drastically cutting its own emissions, lessening its environmental impact. And if that's not enough, Jeff Immelt recently found himself standing in front of Congress urging lawmakers to pass laws that set tougher standards for emissions. To find out more about GE and its involvement in our world, visit: **www.ge.com.**

So I guess instead of asking, "How do you view the world?" I must ask,

How do you view the world now that you have embraced a cause?

Before we get too far along here, how about a little example to help you with the question above? You up for it? Good. Let's play this out a little bit.

Tony used to drive by housing developments and smile. He'd see a strip mall going up and get all warm and fuzzy. A bulldozer would be tearing into a hillside and he'd wonder how he could get a piece of that action. He saw it all as progress which he had learned at business school, was what you wanted. Along the way, the fields that Tony played in as a boy became houses, shops, factories, etc. When he went home it just wasn't the same. The air didn't seem to be the same. The open spaces were gone. When he brought his kids home to grandma and grandpa's house they had nowhere to play and pretty soon, Tony became sad. He began looking at new development differently. He began looking at ways in his community to protect what little open space was left. He began to look at the environmental impact of all the new development and it scared him. His world view changed. Business school hadn't taught him what to do when his favorite boyhood trails were gone.

So Tony became an advocate for creating people friendly, environmentally conscious communities. For creating neighborhoods that were good for people, that embraced open spaces where kids could roam and ride their bikes, where families could go and have a picnic and throw frisbees without having to get in the car for an hour. Tony, himself, started leaving the car in the garage and riding a bike on his daily commutes. (And oh, did his view change then…) He began attending city council meetings when he knew the discussions would be focused on new construction within the community. He worked to get himself appointed to the city planning board. And soon, he started to see his work pay off. Soon he started to convince others in the community that making their city livable was a top priority. Land that was slated for development lost its zoning and was purchased by the city for park space, bike and walking paths were added to the city plan. New housing developments were required to add open spaces to their plans, and overall, the people of Tony's city liked it.

Without looking for a cause, Tony found one. It was a cause that hit close to home and it changed his world-view. He began to look at 'progress' as something more than just the bottom line. And through all of it, Tony changed his world. He was satisfied. The place he called home was home again. And his world may have been just his community, his work may not have caused a ripple effect across the countryside, but then again, maybe it did. Maybe someone from another community came to visit. Maybe they liked what they saw. And maybe, just maybe...

And this is how it will be with you. If your cause is animal cruelty you may never look at a slice of bacon or piece of chicken breast the same way. You may only purchase 'free range' animal products. Heck, you might stop buying anything with animal products and you may end up catching the ENTREPRENEURIAL** bug and decide to start a business that promotes only 'animal-free' products.

But, but, but…you must keep in mind. Lots of people will still eat bacon, buy leather shoes, and purchase animal products that come from factory feedlots. You see, your worldview has changed but your neighbor's hasn't. Many people are not going to see the world the way you see it. But some will. Maybe your neighbor will notice

---

Box #16. The Sixteenth Box.
Time to get behind the wheel and drive.
BECOME AN ENTREPRENEUR

Rebels become entrepreneurs. As you work through each of the steps—as you begin to DO SOMETHING—you'll meet people who offer opportunity. You'll realize that there are gaps where certain products don't exist. You'll start to notice the many companies that got started through a caused-based thought processes. You'll start to notice the many companies that already exist who do good and turn a profit.

And another great thing? These caused-based

---

what you're doing but then again, maybe he won't. And you know what? It's okay. That's right. It's okay. Respect everyone's opinion. Respect everyone's worldview. Don't engage in an argument with someone who just wants to argue. What's the point? People's views are what they are. If you set out to change everyone's view to yours, you'll

---

companies are fun to work with and to work at because everyone who is drawn to them comes because they see and feel the mission of that company. They believe in what the company stands for, what it is all about. So, understand that if you have an idea (and not everyone will), if you're driven to DO SOMETHING commercially focused, you must complete the steps outlined in this book. These 5 SIMPLE STEPS are a must for anyone thinking about being an entrepreneur or starting his/her own business. People can be driven to make money, but they can also want it to be worthwhile.

fail right out of the gate. Not because your cause isn't important, but people won't listen if you don't respect where they're coming from. And if someone is digging in their heels, gearing up for an argument, walk away. You'll only dig yourself a hole and create a place for all sorts of negative energy to come and rest. Save your energy, your positive energy for people who are open.

What's this about Fair Trade?

WHO: Ruth DeGolia and Benita Singh, Founders, Mercado Global

WHAT: As college students, Ruth DeGolia and Benita Singh took nine months away from campus to study in Guatemala where they found women struggling to make a living selling traditional handmade craft items. Upon returning to the states, Ruth and Benita decided to '*DO SOMETHING*' to help these Guatemalan women's cooperatives by selling items at fair trade sales on campus. $5000.00 later, 30 women in Guatemala earned wages for a month and 10 girls were enrolled in school for a year. With this success, Ruth and Benita saw the potential to help not only Guatemalan women, but disadvantaged women from all over the world. In 2004 they launched Mercado Global, a non-profit organization that sells handmade items from women's cooperatives at fair trade prices. And to top it off, Mercado Global fundraises to cover its overhead costs so that it can donate 100% of its profits back to communities around the world. To learn more about Mercado Global, fair trade practices, their partners and their initiatives, visit:

www.mercadoglobal.org.

Little Thing 3: Accept things

I told you it wouldn't be long now, didn't I? You've arrived. The final part to the final step. Take a deep breath. All you have to do now is ACCEPT things. In fact, I could also call this last little exercise, PATIENCE. You'll need it, a lot of it. If my mom were talking to you, she'd tell you to 'put your patience cap on.' And, to get comfortable wearing it.

As we finish up here, there's really no question to be asked, nothing to ponder, no reflecting to be done *(Well, you might want to reflect a little bit...)* But in terms of a big question, well, there isn't one. So you're asking yourself, "Now what am I gonna do?" Well, as you close the cover to this book and set forth ***DOING SOMETHING***, you're going to be patient. Positively patient. You must. If you take a moment to think about it, a whole lot of people have taken a whole lot of years to screw things up. Smog and pollution didn't just happen overnight. War has been with us since the beginning of time. Corrupt businesspeople have been around as long as there has been a buck to be made. People have formed bad habits and practiced them, over and over, for decades, centuries, millenniums. They are ingrained in our collective psyche. And this is why you must have patience.

But you must also have acceptance. You must accept that the world will heal, but it will heal slowly. All the positive energy that you have expended and will expend is being put to good use. You may feel that it's hard to quantify, but it's working. Should you succumb to frustration and begin to feel hopeless, your energy may turn out to be wasted. Remain positive. Change is a turtle. Its moves are purposeful but slow, slow, slow, slow, slow. Look how long it has taken for people to realize that what the large food corporations are processing and selling really isn't good for them. It has taken decades, but the organics industry is finally booming. Even though it still makes up only

2% of food sales it continues to grow and grow because people are devoted to seeing it succeed. People know that encouraging sustainable farming techniques is good for the earth which in turn makes it good for people and future generations.

And look how long it has taken for people to realize that smoking isn't all that healthy and that maybe nonsmokers shouldn't have to be subjected to it? And how many years have we been working on race relations in our country? And feeding the poor and the hungry? And, and…you see? Progress in all of these areas has been made, but progress is often times slow.

And so too is healing. Healing takes time. Healing takes patience—positive patience. Healing takes love. It takes compassion. And it needs you and your small steps—one footprint at a time. And yes, when you really stop and take the time to look at the process of change and healing in the world, you will be truly amazed at how much time it takes to actually see a movement gain traction. But don't let this discourage you or shy you away from it. Understand that once this ball of energy gets rolling, its momentum becomes powerful. As it moves along its energy increases and becomes unstoppable. This energy, this *positive* energy, the energy of change, attracts more and more people to its captivating light. And more and more energy is created and more word of mouth gets going and the big ol' ball keeps growing and moving and shaking things up.

You see, when you set out to heal the world, when you understand that you can actually **DO SOMETHING**, you will heal the world eventually. And the bonus part? You will also heal yourself. Think back for a moment. Remember back to the introduction? The world begins within you, which means, the healing begins within you too. And as you begin to make changes in your life, as you **CHOOSE** and **MOVE** and

NETWORK and *EMBRACE* and finally *UNDER-STAND*, you will begin to heal. And the healing that you'll experience will have a snowball effect. It'll be contagious. Your healing will begin to heal others who will begin to heal others…

And the healing is a beautiful thing.

So go now, begin the healing process.

DO SOMETHING.

And know that you are not alone.

A NOTE OF ENCOURAGEMENT FOR THE STILL UNDECIDED

*Well, you've done it. You've read the book. You're ready to move on but you're not quite sure just what your cause is yet. Maybe you're fascinated by the idea of **DOING SOMETHING** but still overwhelmed about getting started. Even though you'd like to help out, the whole concept of changing the world still seems like a huge undertaking. Or, maybe your list is too long and you're having trouble deciding. You have so many causes you're interested in* *that you'd feel like you're sacrificing some if you focused on just one. Or, maybe your list hasn't filled itself out completely. You've got a few things down but none of them really yanked on the tip of your pencil. None of them have grabbed your thoughts completely and won't let go. So, what are you going to do?*

*First off, know that it's okay. That's right. It's okay. It's okay to be undecided. It's okay to be overwhelmed. It's okay to know that you want to **DO SOMETHING** and just not know what it is yet. You may not find your cause right away. You may not want to choose just one. Or, you may feel more comfortable simply **DOING SOMETHING** quietly in your community. Heck, you might be so busy with school, your latest project at work, or your kids at home that you have no idea where you'd ever fit anything else in.*

So, here's what I want you to do. Take a step back. Take a deep breath. Set the book down. Go for a walk. Go shopping. Take someone you care about out for a bite to eat.

Leave the book behind and let all those unruly thoughts simmer in your head for awhile. And when you're ready, come back to it. When will that be? Who knows? But you will. You'll know when the time is right. For now, however, just let things be.

*And here's what I'm going to do. I'm going to tell you a little story about someone who up and **DID SOMETHING**. Not anything big, but something she could do in a couple of hours, that helped the world around her. I'm also going to give you a few suggestions about what you can do even if you're not sure what it is you want to do.*

WHO: Natalie Parsons, runner

WHAT: Natalie likes to run. She runs a lot. One of her regular routes follows a section of a road and a trail along a creek that had accumulated a bunch of trash. There was so much trash that she often complained to her friends about how awful it was. She even considered changing her route to avoid it, even though she loved running along that quiet and peaceful section of road and trail. Then one weekend Natalie decided to **DO SOMETHING**. She wasn't about to give up her favorite section of trail, but she also wasn't going to continue running through garbage. So, she hopped into her car, drove over to Wal-Mart, bought an orange vest, some work gloves, a big box of trash bags, and headed to the creek. She spent the next few hours filling trash bag after trash bag. By the time she was done, she couldn't believe how many bags she had filled—so many that she had to call a friend with a truck to help her get them to the landfill. And that was it. She went home. Now, whenever she runs through her favorite section of trail, she feels good and is able to enjoy the fact that anyone else who visits won't have to deal with a mess.

And that's Natalie's story. She saw something that needed fixing and she fixed it. Is pollution a problem along our waterways? Sure. Did Natalie take some action? Yep. Did she join a national anti-pollution organization and start working to end pollution? Nope. She didn't feel like she needed to go that far. Simply cleaning up her little peace of heaven was enough. And if the world had a few thousand more Natalie's out there seeing things that needed to be done and just doing them, those thousand little efforts would sure add up to a lot of good.

You see, you don't always have to **DO SOMETHING** that is long-term to help out. You can **DO SOMETHING** in a morning or an afternoon or an evening, on a Saturday or a Sunday. Shoot, if you're lucky, your company might even offer you paid time off to help out. There are opportunities in every community, both organized and unorganized ones just looking for folks like you to get involved. And if that's not enough, there's always National Volunteer Week, Make-A-Difference Day, National Trails Day, Habitat for Humanity, and the list can go on and on. In fact, you could spend your whole life doing little things and all those little things would sure amount to something. And that wouldn't be such a bad thing, now, would it?

So that's it. You have options. You're not stuck sitting on your hands. You can start the 5 Steps today if you haven't already or take comfort in knowing that you can breathe deeply, take a step back and let things settle in a *bit. And if you so desire, you might want to test the waters and do some little things while you're figuring it all out.*

Questions & Answers with the Authors

How did the idea for this book come to be?

AZ: *A little while back I had lunch with three college students who told me that they felt their hands were tied. They were too overwhelmed by the idea of trying to do something and didn't see how anyone could make a difference. It wasn't as if they didn't want to. It was more like they felt they were too insignificant or powerless. And that's when the wheels started turning*

*for 'Get Ready. Get Set. **DO SOMETHING**.' Soon
after that initial discussion, I had pages of notes scrib-
bled on bright orange paper that we used to frame this
book.*

KS: *Well, I can't take credit for this being my idea,
but while Anthony and I worked on 'How Dog Food
Saved the Earth' we had several discussions about
people who were out there making a difference. At the
time, our focus was much more on entrepreneurs and
companies who get involved inside and outside of
their communities, but there was always an understanding that the folks who started up businesses or
who already had a company up and running were just
regular folks who saw their business not only as an
opportunity to make a profit, but to also do something
good in the world. I think some of those discussions led
to a lot of what we did with this book.*

How did you develop the 5 Steps?

AZ: Originally, the 5 Steps were 9 Steps. In my first, really rough draft of the book, I added steps as I wrote without thinking too much about how many there were. I just got my ideas down on paper. I just wrote as fast as I could so I didn't lose my momentum or my ideas. When I step back and really look at where the steps come from, I'd have to say they come from my experiences getting involved in the field of organic food and sustainable farming. Over the years I've used them to help promote the cause of organics.

KS: The first time I heard anything about the steps was when Anthony handed me a stack of orange papers. There were ideas flying all around those papers. As I started to sift through them, I was not only moved by their power, but realized how simple they were to put into action. I also realized that I had unknowingly used a few of them on and off throughout my life. After we *started working at making the book one cohesive unit, we realized that 9 Steps were too many. We didn't want to overwhelm anyone, especially someone who might already seem overwhelmed by the whole idea of trying to make a difference. The best part, however, is that several of the steps blended nicely together and worked better together than they did separately.*

Have you 'DONE SOMETHING'?

AZ: *About 17 years ago, I got angry about modern day, commercialized farming. I had been working in the food industry and was exposed to the ugly side of food production. I couldn't believe the amount of chemicals that were sprayed on fields and crops. I couldn't believe what was added to animal feed and hated the way live- stock was being treated. It made me sick. And I knew that the additives used in processed food might be good for the bottom line, but that was about it. I didn't want to be part of an industry that sold unhealthy food to the general public, especially children. So, I started learning all I could about organics and sustainable farming and headed down that path. Since then, I've started a handful of companies and developed a bunch of products that encourage sustainability, with the Pet Promise line of pet foods being on of the most successful in changing the way farm animals are raised. I'm also the Board Chair at the Organic Center which provides the science behind the benefit of organic agriculture.*

KS: I don't really have a defining moment in terms of wanting to 'Do Something.' As a kid, we were always taught to look out for others and to do the right thing. My parents were active members in our community which made my sisters and I active members in our community. As I got older and college came into view, I realized that the best way for me to get involved and have an impact would be in the classroom. And that's where I ended up for more than a decade. I guess that's ultimately where I found one of my main causes—literacy.

Encouraging others to read what they love and write about what's important to them is definitely a passion of mine. And in terms of importance in our changing world, literacy really is a major key to success.

How much of an impact can the average person have on the world?

AZ: *A huge one. That's why we wrote this book. We want the average person to really be encouraged, to really see that he or she can have an impact. We want them to get out and get involved. Can you imagine the shape our world would be in if everyone got out in our world and got involved with something they really cared about? We would solve all the problems. Collectively, humans are the most powerful beings on Earth. Unfortunately, people consider themselves insignificant when in reality we all have the ability to make some powerful changes.*

KS: *I think our fast-paced modern day society has gotten in the way of people getting involved. It's easy to come home after a long day and do nothing, and obviously, some days you have to. But we're not in total ruins just yet. I see a lot of activity in my local community and nationwide that gives me hope. I haven't had to look much farther than my neighborhood, to find someone who's working on a cause. And I haven't had to look very hard in our local business community to find the same thing. And the people in my community are just average people. Good, average, hard-working people who see a need and try their best to fill it. So yes, I believe the average person can have a huge impact and inspire others also.*

If you could have one wish come true with the message of this book, what would it be?

AZ: *My one wish would be that our book creates a groundswell of people who step outside of their normal, daily routines and begin doing something. And that this groundswell of action creates a huge ripple effect that can be felt all across the world to the point where doing the right thing is commonplace and everyone can see the benefits of a world that works to do good.*

KS: *My one wish is pretty much in line with Anthony's. I'd love to see the whole world working together for the common good. How beautiful and powerful would that be?*

ADDENDUM 1—
MISSION: PERSONAL.

Now that you've made the decision to **DO SOME-THING** for the world, it's probably a pretty good time to step back, take a deep breath and **DO SOMETHING** for yourself—something really important. The ideas in the following addendum — **Mission: Personal**—were first introduced in a book titled, *The Detachment Paradox* (ASM Books, 2004) and further discussed in a follow-up workbook, *The Detachement Paradox: The Workbook* (ASM Books,

2005). We believe so strongly in these activities—in an individual's need to chart his/her own course—that we've taken a few of the gems from those books, dusted them off and polished them up just for you and your own self-awareness, enlightenment, growth, or whatever you might like to call it. Please know, we have used these practical activities in our own lives, at work, at school, and at play, and that we continue to do so today. When you sit down to do them, under-stand that even though they are work, they do work. They've **DONE SOMETHING** powerful for each of us and countless others. If you give them a chance, they will **DO SOMETHING** for you too.

What are you going to do when you grow up?
What are you going to do with your life?
Do you know where you're headed?
Or what you're all about?
Or who you are?

How many times have you asked yourself a question like this? Bet you can't count the number of times. We all have. But when it comes down to it, those aren't the real questions. The real question is, how many times have you actually sat down and started to figure them out? How many times have you given them the time that they deserve? Bet you *can* count the number of times you've given yourself permission to sit down and do some focused thinking about your future. You see, most of us go about our daily lives guided by outside forces. We succumb to the adage, 'Life is what happens to you while you are making other plans.' Yes, I see the twinkle in your eye and the smirk on your face. You know, on a personal level, how easy it is to get sucked up in your daily routine and BOOM, all of a sudden, three months have passed and then six months and then a year and then five years and you look back and wonder where all that time went.

Think about it for a second. How many times have you actually looked at your future and come up with a plan? Even if you have known for a long time what your career path has been, have you ever seriously looked at how those plans affect the rest of your life? Most of us get so caught up in our daily schedules that we don't take the time to step back and reflect. Somehow cleaning the toilets, getting the oil changed, and watching tv takes precedence over planning for our futures. It's unfortunate, but it happens. The good news is, it's never too late (or too early, for that matter) to create a plan for the rest of your life. So we return to our question above:

Will you make the time to look forward and back and decide to become the director of your own destiny?

We hope so.

Okay, let's get on with it. When you ask yourself the questions listed at the beginning of this addendum, and it doesn't matter if you are 16 or 56, and take the time to answer them, you begin a process of self-realization that can only enhance your life's journey. You **DO SOMETHING** for yourself—quite possibly the most important thing you'll ever do for yourself. You see, these questions allow you to take charge of your life. They allow you to stop wandering from one thing to another. And once you stop wandering and

---

In this addendum, 'Mission: Personal' you will:

- **Discover yourself through a 'Personal Audit.'**

- **Create your own 'Personal Mission.'**

begin to take charge, you will create a life that not only encourages but allows you to be happier and healthier. And we like 'happier and healthier'...a lot!

As you begin this process, you'll need to set aside a block of time. An hour or so should be enough to get you started. Once the initial work is done you'll want to come back to this exercise, maybe once, maybe many times. Most likely, you'll dig up so much stuff that you simply won't be able to give all of it your full attention. Don't, however, let this stop you from getting started. This initial process is not only necessary but also incredibly powerful in and of itself and once it is completed you will have many of the tools needed to continue your growth. The other 'stuff' that you don't get to will 'simmer' quietly on the back burner of your mind. Some of it will float to the top. Some of it won't. As time moves along, it will become clear to you which of the 'stuff' demands extra attention and which 'stuff' doesn't. Just have patience. Some of it may take a while for you to understand.

When you begin to work through the **Personal Audit** exercise—and you will find it to be work, good work, but work nonetheless—you'll begin to lay the groundwork for the important work of defining yourself and creating a **Personal Mission Statement**. Once you've completed these tasks, you'll see how important they are in creating a unique **Vision** of your life.

Many successful people have admitted that while they've written successful mission and vision statements for their companies, they've never taken the time or effort to write one for themselves. And these are 'successful' people. Why? The answer is quite simple—most people struggle when asked to define themselves. It feels threatening. It forces them to look not only at their strengths, but also at their shortcomings. It forces them to be honest with themselves. Discovering what represents the real you requires time and patience. You must set aside some time to look within yourself without the distractions of everyday living. And this is not easy in today's world of e-mails, text messaging, and cell phones. It is, however, a crucial step toward living a happier and healthier live and personal fulfillment.

Your Personal Audit

Answer the following questions as honestly as you can. Keep in mind that this is a journey of self-discovery. It may be difficult or even painful, but stay with it. Don't edit yourself. If it pops into your head, write it down, even if it feels a bit uncomfortable. Nobody has to look at your answers except for you. If you get bogged down, move on to the next question. Come back to the more difficult questions later.

What are you passionate about?

_____

_____

_____

_____

With whom or what do you most identify?

_____

_____

_____

_____

What are your strengths at work or school? Outside of work or school?

_____

_____

_____

_____

What are your weaknesses at work or school? Outside of work or school?

_____

_____

_____

Do you feel stifled? If so, why?

_____

_____

_____

_____

Do you live for the weekends? If so, why?

_____

_____

_____

_____

What words, expressions or quotes do you find particularly inspiring?

_____

_____

_____

_____

What are you good at—either personally, scholarly, or professionally?

_____

_____

_____

What are your inner resources? Are you, or controlling forces in your life, keeping them from emerging?

_____

_____

_____

_____

What words best describe you?

_____

_____

_____

What identifies and connects everyone around you in a common and worthy pursuit?

_____

_____

_____

_____

What seeds of greatness or ingenuity might you be harboring, and how far have you gone towards cultivating them?

_____

_____

_____

Do you want to be part of something that can make the world a better place?

_____

_____

_____

Go back and look at your answers for questions 1-13. Is there an underlying theme connecting your answers? Can you see what is most important to you? Take a few moments and write any further thoughts you have regarding yourself and your personal audit.

_____

_____

_____

As you reflect back over the last 14 questions, there may have been a few that were difficult for you to answer. Remember, this is a process which should take some time. Don't forget those questions. Instead, let them float around in your subconscious and come back to them in the near future.

What is a 'Personal Mission'?

Quite simply stated, a personal mission is a person's true calling. It is the discovery of what represents the 'real you.' It is 'what you are all about.' A personal mission is a person's internal compass. Look to it in order to find direction.

We all need direction in life. In fact, we are all following one path or another. The question is, then, whose path are you following? Are you under your own direction or is someone else charting your course?

The following exercises will help you discover your personal mission. It is designed to be a *process— one that you will want to come back to.* Take your time.

1. On the longer line, list words that describe what you would do with your life if school or money or career were not an issue. (e.g. "build," "create," "encourage," "activate," "educate," "manage" etc.) Do your best to write an 'action' type word on each line. (See the following list for ideas.)

— _____   — _____

— _____   — _____

— _____   — _____

— _____   — _____

— _____   — _____

— _____   — _____

Here are some words to get you started: challenge, urge, sell, encourage, inspire, excite, conquer, impress, gain, give, love, move, help, relax, go, uplift, laugh, listen, learn, nurture, lead, plan, accept, change, mentor, create, entice, share, travel, motivate, teach, exercise, play, read, support.

2. Now, list the types of endeavors—social, scholarly, cultural, organizational, spiritual, or business-related—that most 'turn you on' (e.g. "music," "art," "health," "motivation," "public service," "education," "environmental protection," etc.) List at least 10 of them.

__ _____   __ _____

__ _____   __ _____

__ _____   __ _____

__ _____   __ _____

__ _____   __ _____

3. Next, go back to your first list. Circle your top "10." These are the ones that jump off the page at you. Then, using the short lines, put these top "10" in order from "1 to 10." The "1" will be the one that hits you at your core. It speaks to you the loudest. It is a part of you, whether or not you have ever recognized it before today.

4. Finally, go back to your second list. Circle the top "5" that you identify with most. Number them from "1 to 5." The "1" will represent that which is of most importance to you.

5. Look back at your lists. Take a few words from your top "10" and put them together in a sentence along with a word or two from your top "5." Define your mission. Write at least four versions using a mixture of your top words in the activity boxes on pages 186 and 187.

6. After you have written a few, go back and circle the one that jumps off the page. Write it in the bottom box on page 187.

(Please note: The activities presented here are intended to get you started on your way to understanding yourself more. For a more in depth discussion regarding personal missions

---

Personal mission vs. Professional mission

"What if my personal mission has nothing to do with my professional life or the path I have chosen in school?"

In order for you to lead a fulfilling, rewarding life, you must first define yourself. In defining yourself, you give yourself direction. Once you have given yourself direction, you can begin to assess the other facets of your life to see if they are in alignment with your mission.

including activities to help you create a plan for your future and creating time to do it all please check out Exercise 1, pages 21-43l in The Detachment Paradox: How an objective approach to work can lead to a rich and rewarding life (ASM Books, 2004) and Section 1, pages 4-20, in The Detachment Paradox: The Workbook.(ASM Books, 2004) or visit: www.detachmentparadox.com and/or www.asmbooks.com.)

You may find that there are parts of your life that do not align—your job or the path you have chosen in school for instance. And as frustrating as this may seem at the time, it is a crucial step in looking towards your future. With this new found knowledge of yourself, you can begin to look in other areas of your life, research new possibilities, and lay the groundwork for meaningful change. You can begin to redefine your life and hopefully merge your personal mission with your profession or schooling sometime down the road.

(Here are a couple of examples—
although yours may be entirely different.)

My mission is to…laugh with others, build positive personal relationships, and motivate those in my life to do the same.

My mission is to…laugh with others, build positive personal relationships, and motivate those in my life to do the same.

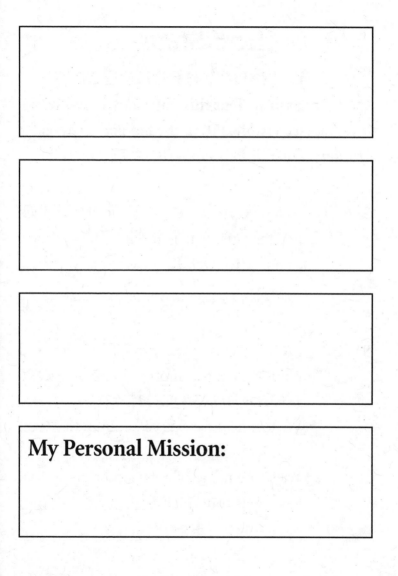

My Personal Mission:

The 5 Steps— A Visual Reminder

Instructions: Tear this out. Copy it. Put it someplace visible. Fill in the blanks as you go.
(Remember, it helps to write things down...)

STEP 1.   *CHOOSE.* Choose a cause. Just one. Pick one that speaks to you. Take a stand. Make a choice. *CHOOSE.*

Write your cause here: _____

STEP 2.   *MOVE.* Get moving with information and reinforcements. Inform yourself. *MOVE IT! MOVE IT! MOVE IT!*

Write one great piece of info that you have learned: _____

Write the name of a person or group you have met/ contacted: _____

STEP 3. *NETWORK.* Participate with your selected group. Be involved. ***NETWORK.***

Write one way that you are getting involved: _____

STEP 4. ***EMBRACE.*** What can you personally do to ***EMBRACE*** your cause? How will you include it in your life? _____

Write one way that you have embraced your cause?_____

STEP 5. *UNDERSTAND.* Change takes time. What do you see changing so far?_____

Write one thing, even the tiniest thing, that you have seen change, either about yourself or your cause. _____

ACKNOWLEDGEMENTS

Anthony would like to say...

This book is a collection of many people's gifts of thoughts and insights over the years. Everyone that comes into my life seems to have shared ideas or points of view that have shaped my own. So, thanks to all of you who have made this book possible.

I would like to especially thank my parents John and Dolly Zolezzi for providing an environment and an attitude that made me believe that anything is possible, my niece Ellen Bruegge who was the inspiration for the title and content of this book, and Kory Swanson and his wife, Jen Todd who bring the book to life.

Again, a special gratitude goes out to all the people that I have been so fortunate to meet over the years. Thank you for the gifts of your thoughts and ideas—keep them coming.

Kory would like to say…

I'm absolutely convinced that this book would not have been possible without the seeds my parents, Mary Jo and Gary Swanson, planted early in my life. They taught me to look beyond myself. They taught me to care. To my wife, Jen, who believes in me and encourages me. There's no one I'd rather be sharing my life with.

And thanks to all of you who sat with pen in hand, on your own time, and told us we had something after reading our rough drafts: Nicole Hanson, Rick Hausman, Kimeri Swanson-Beck, Claytie Moorman, Jeff Todd, Jim Hausman, Kari Swanson-Coady, and Andrea Boccacino.

ABOUT THE AUTHORS

Anthony Zolezzi is an eco-entrepreneur and author who has devoted himself to improving humanity and the condition of our planet. He has been responsible for the development of more than 25 entrepreneurial companies and products, all of which have been designed to encourage healthy living and sustainability. Anthony promotes organic agriculture and encourages some of the largest companies in the country to implement sustainable business practices. He has worked with organizations ranging from start-ups to Fortune 500 companies including Nestle, The Prince of Wales, Duchy Originals, Bumble Bee Foods, Horizon Organic Dairy, Wild Oats Markets, Viacom, and Paramount Pictures. In addition, Anthony has taken social trends and turned them into food trends such as his creation of Bubba Gump Shrimp Co. Restaurants based on the award-winning film "Forrest Gump" starring Tom Hanks. He also developed Café Nervosa Coffee based off of NBC's hit sitcom, "Frasier."

Anthony is Chairman of the Board for The Organic Center for Education and Promotion. He is author of, "Chemical-Free Kids" (Kensington, 2003), "The Detachment Paradox" (ASM Books, 2004), "The Detachment Paradox: The Workbook" (2004) and "How Dog Food Saved the Earth" (ASM Books, 2005).

Kory Swanson plays with words, concerns himself with the human condition, and wants everyone to rediscover the joys of riding a bike. When he is not chasing two kids around the house, feeding Barkley the desert tortoise, or bouncing ideas around with his wife, Jennifer, about how to better instruct high school kids, he sits at the computer trying to make sense of the world through the written word. In a previous life, Kory spent time wandering the halls of public education encouraging our future leaders to clearly express themselves. Now he's encouraging his daughter to express herself without dumping her food all over the kitchen floor.

This is the third time Kory has teamed up with Anthony. He is the author of "The Detachment Paradox: The Workbook (2004) and "How Dog Food Saved the Earth" (ASM Books, 2005).

Other titles by ASM Books

How Dog Food
Saved the Earth

The Detachment Paradox

The Detachment Paradox:
The Workbook

Contact ASM Books
P.O. Box 3083
La Habra, CA 90631
(310) 528 - 2830
www.asmbooks.com